FROM WHERE I WAS STANDING

A LIVERPOOL SUPPORTER'S VIEW
OF THE HEYSEL STADIUM TRAGEDY

CHRIS ROWLAND

FOREWORD BY
PAUL TOMKINS

FROM WHERE I WAS STANDING

CONTENTS

ISBN 978-0-9559253-1-3

Published By GPRF Publishing

First edition published 2009

ACKNOWLEDGEMENTS

My thanks to Chris Hadley for the work and guidance that went into proofing the final manuscript.

Thanks to the group of Liverpool supporting mates who appear in this book, many of whom still have Kop season tickets. Over more than thirty years we've shared a lot of triumph and joy, fun and laughter, despair and, on two occasions, disaster.

Thanks of course to Paul Tomkins for writing the foreword and providing the support, encouragement and opportunity to give this work the chance to fly.

Finally, thanks to Hils for her patience and support throughout the book's lengthy gestation period.

FOREWORD

Heysel and Hillsborough: the twin H-bombs of Liverpool FC's history.

While the latter event has been analysed in books, TV documentaries and as part of countless fan campaigns and protests, the former remains an almost unacknowledged spectre; the elephant in the room. Whereas Hillsborough involved nothing but innocent match-going behaviour by the fans, the events of Heysel remain less clear-cut, falling into the murky waters of *manslaughter*: something we all risk day after day, when we accept a mobile phone call while driving or take our eyes off the road to fiddle with the stereo.

No-one set out to kill anyone, and were it not for a stadium that looked like it was built at the time of the Romans (only with far less skill and durability), an unsavoury evening would have remained just that. Instead, thanks to a number of pitfalls with the stadium and the event organisation, it became the largest-profile game ever to end in disaster, as 39 Italians tragically lost their lives. Nick Hornby, the noted author and Arsenal supporter, once wrote that what Liverpool fans did — charge at their rival's numbers — was part and parcel of English football culture at the time. Only this time it had serious consequences.

Over the years I have been approached by quite a few writers, interested in my help with getting their work published, but what they propose has rarely appealed to me: some ideas overlap with the work I produce, while other concepts just aren't interesting enough. This project was different, and instantly caught my attention: after all, this book documents a piece of history, written at the time.

Chris' account provides a long-overdue voice for those Liverpool fans who were in Belgium that fateful day. The original manuscript, written in the immediate aftermath of Heysel purely as a form of catharsis (and then left to gather dust), was due to be serialised by the *Liverpool Echo* in 1989; incredibly, the final document landed on the *Echo*'s Sports Desk on the 15th of April of that year. Suffice it to say, events surrounding the club that Saturday, as 96 Liverpool fans lost their lives, overshadowed what had occurred four years earlier, and the serialisation was naturally abandoned. Since then the manuscript has been updated, to take into account events in the interim, and the time seemed right, with the 25th anniversary looming, to get this story to an audience.

Chris' long-standing and deeply committed support of the Reds was also appealing to me in agreeing to get involved with the project. He was no fly-by-night fan at the game in 1985 — this was, and still is, an experienced traveller; one who has attended all ten of Liverpool's European finals since 1973.

And this is his story of how carefree trip to the continent turned into a long dark night in Brussels.

Paul Tomkins
August 2009

CHAPTER 1
PLANNING A JOURNEY

April 1985.

Liverpool Football Club had just won its semi-final to reach the European Cup Final — the summit of European club football. To the victors, the title of Champions of Europe.

Waiting for them was another member of European football's aristocracy, Juventus of Turin.

Despite the two clubs' pre-eminence, they had never before met in European competition. This first encounter was anticipated with great excitement. The venue would be the Heysel Stadium, Brussels; the date May 29th, 1985.

After a 4-0 home victory in the first leg of the semi-final, against Panathinaikos of Athens, qualifying for the final was pretty much a formality. We knew we could now start planning our trip to Brussels. Having been to Liverpool's four previous European Cup finals — twice in Rome, once in Paris and once at Wembley — none of us would even contemplate missing this one.

'We', incidentally, refers to a group of Midlands-based individuals bound together since the early 1970s by our devotion to Liverpool Football Club and our liking for drinking beer, twin predilections that dovetail quite handily. The names of the group members have been changed to preserve their anonymity.

The daily barrage of telephone calls began the very next evening after the semi-final. Long-suffering partners, by now well accustomed to this periodic loss of their menfolk to foreign lands for less than a week but to the telephone for five or six, will sigh with an air of resignation, and wonder with a touch of incredulity just how much planning it takes to go to one football match.

The answer is quite a lot. A surprising amount. Just trying to organise our transport for a routine home game is often difficult and complicated enough, and can take many phone calls. But when the game's abroad and there's accommodation as well as travel to arrange, and when the only fixed factor is that we have to be at the stadium, ideally with a match ticket, in time for kick-off, it becomes a highly complex organisational task, requiring many of the skills that modern employers place high on their competency profiles. In fact it is fair to compare the task to a part-time job: 'Applicants must be prepared to work unpaid for a minimum of 12 hours per week, including evenings and weekends, showing commitment, enthusiasm, dogged persistence and the patience of a saint. You will be dealing with some members of the group who resolutely remain uninvolved in the whole process until, having led completely normal, blissfully untroubled lives for the last few weeks, they finally manage to raise a telephone about three days before the ferry sails or the plane starts to taxi, to ask "What are we doing then, is everything sorted?"

'Is everything sorted?', a superficially innocent question, is actually a form of verbal shorthand. What it's short for is: 'Can you give me a comprehensive breakdown of everything you've been arranging on my behalf for the last few weeks, as you nearly disappear up your own backside whilst your own normal life suffers its very own comprehensive breakdown?' It means: 'Have you booked the train/ferry/accommodation, have we got match tickets yet, what time do I need to be at the station, how much cash should I bring and do I need to bring sandwiches?' Oh, and perhaps with current exchange rates and the Channel weather forecast thrown in. They seem to have no idea how much work is involved, but in reality probably do. For the organisers, it's maddening. Of course, knowing that it's maddening only heightens their joy at seeing you being maddened.

You may sense by now that I was one of the organisers. As anyone who has ever served on a committee will testify, organisational workloads have a habit of ending up in the same few hands, which is fine if they're not yours. But they usually are mine. Perhaps I am a control freak who can't bear the thought of leaving arrangements to others who couldn't possibly do it as well as me. Besides, everyone thinks I'm 'sensible', a confidence-crushing tag if ever there was one. It speaks of pragmatic shoes, anoraks and mildly eccentric hobbies like sand-collecting or moth-watching. After all, women don't want sensible, do they? Women are not excited by a guy who would never allow a library book to become overdue. Women want danger, unpredictability, maybe even mild latent menace. They want moody and brooding, like Clint Eastwood in *A Fistful of Dollars*. Not sensible. At least I think they do. Who bloody knows?

But sensible is ideal for organising trips. Mobilising this disparate bunch for overseas manoeuvres and moulding it into a well-knit unit that arrives at the right places at the right times with all its correct paperwork is indeed a quasi-military task of testing proportions. The trouble is, each one has a vote, and each has the power of veto. And to state the obvious, you can't actually go ahead and make travel and accommodation arrangements unless you can all agree where and how you're going. Sounds simple? It should be. But do eight people ever agree on anything? Do eight people all choose exactly the same meals from a menu? Do they all like their tea the same way? It's not so easy, there's always someone with a special requirement that doesn't dovetail with the rest. And each laborious step, each development in each of the key stages — dates, times, places, budgets and match tickets — has to be relayed to seven other people, for their agreement. Or not.

Meanwhile, the balls-aching task of chiselling out precious match tickets must begin. You start by contacting everyone you know who has contacts. You shake as many branches as possible and hope that a precious ticket will eventually flutter gently, sweetly earthwards into your clutching, grasping mitts. It's competitive, getting your name on a ticket, and time-consuming. It seems a little blunt to ring somebody you don't speak to that often and then just say: "By the way, any chance of a ticket for the final mate?" So you ask how the kids/wife/job are, about their life generally, before slipping in the question, but they know what you're calling for and they're waiting for it, and besides you're only the fifth that night alone to call to enquire how the wife/kids/job are.

For anyone who doesn't know, the life of the hallowed match ticket for these major football occasions begins when the governing body, UEFA, decides on the venue, the capacity of which will dictate the total number of tickets available. UEFA then decides how those tickets will be distributed, using a formula that makes solving the human genome seem comparatively straightforward. It usually defies logic, but at least the outcome is usually consistent — too few tickets go to the two clubs involved, and never anything like enough to go round. And so it was on this occasion. The two clubs would receive around 15,000 tickets each, with demand far outstripping supply at both. Apply simple market forces and hey presto, you have fierce competition, inflated prices, a buoyant black market, people travelling without tickets and all the attendant security risks. It's inevitable, as night follows day, and it's about time the authorities stopped mouthing platitudes about the problems that inevitably follow. You can't sow seeds and then complain that they grow.

Given the Heysel Stadium's capacity of approaching 50,000 at the time, you immediately marvel at where all those other tickets go. It's the same with domestic cup finals; the sponsors, the dignitaries and officials, whoever they are, the corporate fat cats and god knows who else, all have first go in the trough. When they are sated, the real fans are allowed to enter the picture — or at least some of them. You know, the ones who supported the club throughout the earlier less glamorous matches, the ones who are praised to the heavens by the clubs' executives and management for their marvellous support when it suits them, and ignored when it doesn't. *Us.*

The baton then passes to the two clubs involved. They each receive their meagre allocation of tickets from UEFA, and have to decide how to distribute them. Liverpool Football Club, as representatives of the hooligan-besmirched English game, would have been especially sensitive to the need for their ticket-selling arrangements to stand up to the closest scrutiny, to be an absolutely watertight, loophole-free zone. Any English club knew then, and still knows today, that the behaviour of its followers abroad would (and will) be under the microscope. The usual platitudes emerge: that only 'genuine' supporters will be able to obtain tickets; anybody without tickets is urged not to travel (which only makes you want to scream 'Well don't make it so bloody difficult to get one then!'), the club goes to great lengths to ensure no tickets end up in the wrong hands, does not condone bad behaviour and dissociates itself from any violence, and so on. But unless you happened to be a director, shareholder, member of the first-team squad or season ticket holder whose serial number happened to end in the right numbers, acquiring a ticket through official channels was all but closed to you. Several of us did not fall into any of those elite categories apart from season-ticket holders, and since the only lucky draw I've ever won was a box of past-their-sell-by-date Cadbury's Animals in my local pub, I wasn't confident about my ticket number being drawn. It wasn't. Your season ticket serial had to end in one of three of the nine possible digits to qualify, and mine didn't. Only two of our group qualified this way. Almost a cull really.

Let's make this clear, right at the outset, because this is one issue that non-football fans keep returning to — fans travelling without tickets. Travelling to a match without a ticket means you'll instantly be prejudged as an irresponsible hooligan hell-bent on looting and pillage by our ranting press, and, at the time, the foaming-at –the-mouth Thatcherite government. And indeed by the supporters of other English clubs hell-bent on some mischief-making of their own, and not missing a chance to pile derision on their rivals. Football clubs, football authorities, police, even governments, are haunted by the spectre of thousands of ticketless fans arriving at a city or stadium, threatening to short-circuit all the elaborate security and crowd segregation measures.

Well, every single supporter would prefer to have one in advance. Nothing beats the peace of mind that comes with leaving these shores with your match ticket tucked safely away in your pocket. But nowhere near everyone who wants a ticket gets one. Those season ticket holders who don't qualify for a ticket can surely be forgiven for wanting one — after all, they've proved their commitment by being there every week and shelling out handsomely for the privilege. The trouble is, you have to make the decision to go to the match long before the ticket allocation and distribution is even known, let alone whether you'll get one or not. It can often be just a few days prior to the game before you find out whether you'll get a ticket or not. By that time, all your travel and accommodation arrangements must have been already made, and probably paid for. So imagine if amongst the eight of us, only five got hold of tickets in advance. Come the day of departure, after all their involvement in the planning, all the anticipation of what is to come, all the hope that a ticket will still turn up, are the other unlucky three really going to cancel it all, back out at the eleventh hour, lamely resign themselves to watching it on telly and lose whatever money they've already paid out? Or do they travel with their mates regardless, hope they can find a ticket en route or at the match, or at worst watch the game in a bar near the ground with many others in the same predicament? At least then they'll be there, feeling part of it, not stuck at home or in the local in front of the telly, which you can do anytime. That's why so many fans will travel anyway, even without a ticket. Because they have to, they're already committed. You know you'll be reviled by your club, the football authorities, the government, probably even your neighbours and work colleagues, for being irresponsible, for not being under control, because they think the only reason you would ever do it this way is because you want to cause trouble. But the bottom line is you'll go anyway, even without a ticket. After all, if the chosen venue isn't big enough, if the allocation of tickets to your club isn't big enough, if the system fails to provide, it's hardly your fault is it?

The way clubs usually try to resolve this issue is to organise official club trips, by coach and by air, attaching a match ticket to the grossly inflated all-inclusive price. Official trips often go straight from airport or railway station or coach park to the ground; you watch the match, and then you go straight back again, with barely a taste of tapas or a scent of the city. They are rarely the last word in comfort, are generally over-regimented and universally overpriced, and at that time alcohol was supposed to be prohibited, although sanctions-busting was not unknown. Even the more luxurious trips, with overnight stays included, are extremely expensive and a little over-organised and sanitised. If you enjoy the experience of being somewhere else, of seeing a foreign city for yourself on your own terms and getting a fleeting snapshot of its life, if you prefer to spend a few days somewhere rather than a few hours, then such trips are not for you. Unfortunately, neither will a match ticket be.

Well I was never one for package holidays, football or otherwise. Funny, but most supporters I know don't actually enjoy being shepherded on and off transport and coerced into subhuman compliance. That's why many choose to make their own arrangements, accepting that the price of their freedom to convert the experience into something akin to a holiday will be several weeks of being more or less fully occupied in organising and securing tickets. The idea is that even if you get the promise of a ticket, you don't stop trying. Once you've got your own, it's just one less to find for the group. You look out for each other. That's the theory anyway, and by and large it works. Football fans have their sense of community and their own strong and rigid set of values, codes and bonds. Your team is your community, and at times a surprisingly caring one. So we put the calls in and prepared for a long, anxious wait.

The next decision was where to base ourselves. You only have to glance at a map to see the obvious contenders. Being the days before cheap flights, we were going by ferry, which landed at either Zeebrugge or Ostend. We instantly dismissed staying in the capital itself — in hindsight one of our better decisions. Too big, too volatile with two sets of supporters, too competitive for rooms. And who knew what the locals and the police would be like? Alternatively, it could be so fearful and security-conscious that everything would be closed — at least to us — and just waiting for the match to be over and the supporters to leave before normal life resumed.

So Ghent, or Antwerp? Both lovely cities, both easy to travel to and from, both free of the pressures of the match venue itself. My sensible vote went for the culture of chocolate box-cover Bruges, all pretty canals and stunning Flemish architecture, and only a short hop from the ferry. It was instantly swamped in a tidal wave of support for coarser, brasher, livelier Ostend, the Belgian Blackpool. Being sensible, I had to concede that it made sense. Only sixty or so miles from Brussels, well served by trains, handy for the ferry. We studied ferry timetables and prices, and those modern-day hieroglyphics known as European train timetables. Fortunately we had our own rail employee, Phil, to interpret. He understands these things. The embryo of a plan began to form. At which point, a logistical spanner was hurled into the works, and it went by the name of Vince. Vince is to smooth organisation what Genghis Khan was to village fetes. Veteran of many a European campaign he may be, but never underestimate the power of this diminutive bandy-legged scouser-in-exile to sabotage your carefully laid plans.

The excited phone call came one evening. "You won't believe this!" said Vince. "I've only won a lucky draw at my local travel agent. It's a three day spring mini-break for two — in Belgium! To be taken by the end of May 1985. Perfect timing or what?" To what must have been the unrestrained joy of his then-wife, he had selected me as his lucky partner.

Right dates, right country even. It seemed too perfect. I was interested, but I must admit a little hesitant at first. I'm not one to look a gift horse, or indeed a free prize horse, in the mouth, but this one came with Vince attached. Experience urged caution. But showing poor judgment for one so sensible, I finally decided that free B&B for three nights and free travel from London Victoria to Ostend were too good to miss. Not to mention the sheer adrenalin rush of a 5% reduction in admission to the Dolphinarium and a free glass of wine in a pizza joint in the red light district. 'The services of our resident hostesses' sounded more enticing though. More of them later too, and none of it good.

The original plan had been for all eight of us to travel to Ostend on the Tuesday, stay Tuesday and Wednesday nights and return to England on the Thursday. Accommodating our prize would mean Vince and I travelling a day earlier, ahead of the other six. I pictured a civilised-ish Monday evening, sitting in the residents' lounge sipping cocktails and nibbling canapés, and taking Tuesday breakfast in smoking jackets in the conservatory, before the others arrived on Tuesday, when the whole occasion would revert to its usual feral nature as they scoured the less prepossessing parts of town for burgers, chips and cheap rooms.

They greeted news of the free prize with incredulity: 'You'll regret it'; 'It'll end in chaos'; and 'It is with Vince you know, when will you ever learn?' There were also dark mutterings about it being bad form travelling separately and not sticking together, but we just dismissed that as envious pique, and quietly hoped they weren't right. After all, it was a prize, what could go wrong?

I'm still not sure how a relationship with a travel agent can deteriorate so badly. It began straightforwardly enough, with a misunderstanding over dates. The travel agent, who in all fairness to Vince is not to be recommended, informed Vince that the Wednesday evening was not available. That being the night of the match, it was the one we needed most. The agent said Vince had given him the wrong dates or something. Vince was adamant he hadn't. You get the picture. To be fair to Vince, it's unlikely he'd get the date of the European Cup Final wrong. So they started swapping sarcasm, then insults. Over the following days, every possibility for a misunderstanding was fully exploited, and there unfolded an impenetrable sequence of verbal sparring and indelicate exchanges, relayed to me nightly by an increasingly irate and entrenched Vince. The outcome was we lost Monday evening as well. Only Tuesday left.

The sorry saga soon degenerated into a salvage operation. Meanwhile if the rest of the group, whose own arrangements were by comparison simplicity itself, tried in any way to avoid saying: 'Told you so' and gloating, they failed utterly, instead parading the barely disguised smugness of those who've been right all along. Each night, during the course of yet another update call, 'Any news on tickets?' (answer no) would inevitably be followed with: 'Er … how's the mini-break coming along?', before collapsing into laughter.

Vince and I decided to cut our losses — I was in no position to do much else, it wasn't me who'd won the miserable bloody holiday. Of the dream holiday that oh-so-recently comprised free travel from London and three nights' accommodation in the Hotel Pacific, Ostend, only the free travel and one night emerged from the wreckage. It was decided we might as well all travel together after all. Trains and ferries could at last be booked, leaving just the troubled issue of match tickets unresolved. Already there were dark rumours of forgeries and sky-high black market prices, and our network of contacts remained stubbornly unproductive. Only ten days to go.

When the breakthrough finally came it was both sudden and unexpected. You tend and nurture your contacts as a farmer his crops, then you just sit back and wait anxiously for it to bear fruit. The failure rate is high. But as, one by one, all eight tickets came through from various sources, the elation was palpable. A major obstacle was removed, a shadow lifted, and the anticipation could begin in earnest. All the pieces were finally in place.

Phil and I drove to a Coventry pub to collect our tickets. The handful of Monday night regulars paid little attention as eight rare and precious tickets for the European Cup Final and a considerable amount of sterling changed hands. A cursory glance at the tickets, before they were thrust deep inside jacket pockets, revealed them to be dull, drab, unspectacular affairs compared to the glossy works of art produced for our previous finals in Rome (see photographs on page 80). It somehow didn't seem fitting for such a showpiece occasion. Latin flair versus Anglo-Saxon pragmatism.

We looked at the plan of the ground on the reverse of the ticket to see where we would be standing — it's what fans do, with their territorial instincts. This spot of reconnaissance showed that our terrace tickets were for Block XYZ, behind one goal, whilst Juventus' supporters would presumably be behind the other at the opposite end, Block ONM.

Note that Block Z on the tickets had been overprinted with a big black blob. We took that to be for crowd segregation purposes, perfectly normal procedure at the time at every match at home, to which we English fans had long since grown accustomed. It scarcely seemed worthy of note. We assumed it meant that either Block Z would be empty, or if not then neutral and separated from us in Blocks X and Y by barbed wire, high steel fencing and a significant percentage of the Belgian police force.

But when ten nights later, almost to the minute, thirty-nine lives were lost in the mangled debris in the corner of Block Z, it was not empty, but filled with rival Juventus supporters, and separated from X and Y by nothing more substantial than a chest-high stretch of chicken wire more suited to the allotment than the European Cup Final. Had we known, there and then in that Coventry pub, that Block Z would be full of rival supporters and barely segregated, we could have told anybody who cared to listen that this was a very dangerous arrangement and not one to take chances with. That it would lead to problems was wholly foreseeable as well as easily preventable. We would have known it instantly. UEFA and the Heysel Stadium management already knew it, but for reasons that have still never been explained, chose to disregard it.

CHAPTER 2
A BIT ABOUT FOOTBALL, AND A BIT OF HISTORY

Many so-called experts and analysts glibly compare football with 'rival leisure activities' such as going to the cinema, a restaurant or a concert. If football fails to remain competitive against these rivals for the 'leisure pound', they argue, the 'customers' will 'vote with their feet' and go to the cinema instead.

This shows a breathtaking lack of understanding. It misses the central point utterly. You don't 'support' a cinema, a restaurant or a music venue, you just go there to passively consume. You don't support any particular supermarket, despite their best attempts to make you a 'fan' through loyalty cards, bonus points or whatever incentive they can come up with next. There are no heated Showcase v UCI debates, no Tesco and Morrison fans goading each other over trading results, yoghurt prices or strawberry quality. You may have a preference, but it's nothing stronger than that. And would you keep going to a restaurant where the food is poor, week after week? Well a football fan keeps going to watch his or her team, no matter how poorly it's performing. He does not 'vote with his feet', by going to watch another team — normally the whole basis of market forces. His allegiance is not transferable, ever. His support is as much duty as leisure choice. How his team is performing is not the basis of his allegiance, although it will certainly colour his outlook on life in general — at least until the next match. He is not a consumer. He is a supporter of his team. Totally different things. Emotionally tied in, personally involved, bonded for life, for richer and for poorer, sharing the emotions and the customs of thousands of like-minded fans. Supporting a football team is not the same thing as going to watch a game of football.

In this lifelong strength of the bond between club and followers, football is I believe unique (although I can already hear the rumblings of dissent from fans of rugby, cricket, ice hockey and so on). When you hear fans refer to 'we' when they talk about their club, it's because they feel part of the club. They *are* part of the club, and arguably the most important part. After all, only they and the stadium are constant (new stadia disregarding), the only continuum connecting the generations. Players and managers come and go, but fans are there for life. I was there watching long before Ian Rush made his debut, and I'm still there long after he's ceased playing. Fans expect and hope that players and managers will show loyalty, but fans show it always. The fans are the thread, the lifeline. If ever that connection between club and supporter is lost, so will football be, for it will have become just another commodity, subject to passing prevailing whims and market forces.

That's not to say football is incapable of losing paying support from its stadia. Many factors can contribute to that, with cost right at the top of the list. There is also growing disaffection with over-hyped, overpaid prima donna players and altered kick-off times to accommodate live TV. There is a growing number of TV pub fans, excluded from being there by either price or the impossibility of getting tickets, or both.

Football support is often described as tribal, and there's some substance in that. But there's another entirely appropriate term, not as overblown as may first appear — the religious term 'devotion'. For are there not many similarities between organised religion and following a football team, even extending to the vocabulary? Is the stadium not the church, where the congregation gathers to sing, praise and worship together, sharing but one single common faith? A congregation of a size any church could only dream of becomes one voice, the way to eternal bliss barred only by the evil foe, the unbelievers, the opposition, who must be vanquished if glory is to prevail. The whole match day experience is studded with quasi-religious ritual, from the chants and wearing of colours proclaiming allegiance to a whole shared history. Away games become a crusade, to spread the word amongst the infidel barbarians.

During more than a hundred years of football in England, each club has evolved into its own entire mini-religion, complete with its own unique customs, its own belief and value systems — and its own demons. And to truly belong, you must espouse unquestioningly the tenets and traditions of your particular cause, just like a religion. The team's victory is your victory, its defeat your defeat. There's no need to try to explain to any of your fellow believers how you feel because they already know. For a precious few moments, you are understood, you are not inarticulate, and you are definitely not alone. This can be an exciting, exquisite, sublime, heady, adrenalin-fuelled, wondrously uplifting release from mundane everyday life, from home, from work, from relationships, from sheer daily monotony. Few will derive such sensations from any other activity in their lives.

By 1985, Liverpool's European triumphs and adventures had become deeply and richly embedded in the club's heritage, a source of immense pride, in the club and, through it, in yourself. You shone in the reflected glory. At the time, Liverpool was the team to beat, domestically as well as in Europe. Throughout the 1970s and 80s, during the club's twenty years of on-field dominance, the supporters of Liverpool Football Club inevitably developed a certain arrogance, not unlike Manchester United's have now, though I would argue nothing like as insufferably! This air of supremacy manifested most acutely in their involvement in European football. The season that culminated in Heysel was Liverpool's twentieth consecutive year of involvement in European competition. In the process they had reached eight European finals and won six major trophies; four of them the big one, the European Cup itself.

As the gathering of all the champion teams across Europe, the European Cup (now the Champions League) was Europe's top footballing trophy, the biggest trophy of all, and not just physically. Winning it makes you European Champions, and hearing that final whistle delivers a buzz and a bursting sense of pride like no other. There is nothing to compare with it, even though winning your domestic league is the truer test of your team's ability. The European Cup was an elite competition for champions only, whereas the Champions League, paradoxically, is not. There were only two ways your team could get into the European Cup

— either by winning your country's domestic league, or by qualifying as holders having won the previous year's European Cup. No second, third or fourth places.

By the time Heysel arrived, Liverpool had won the trophy four times in the previous eight years, and the supporters had formed a special attachment to that tournament and trophy that lives on to this day — witness the totally different atmosphere at Anfield on Champions League nights compared to most league games. The crowd for those tingling European nights is by and large the same people as for the league games, but each individual is acting very differently, because it has come to be expected. They stand, they sing, they believe, they never shut up. It's powerful, emotional, an elevated state of devotion and fervour. The same individuals can be becalmed, passive and critical three days earlier or later for the surrounding league games. Although Liverpool have been English league champions 18 times, its fans reluctantly accept that other English teams will sometimes win it. But other English teams winning the European Cup really hurts. It feels like they're on our territory. It's our turf, it's personal. The league is common ground, open to every team in the top division (in theory), but the European Cup/Champions League is exclusive.

The supporters who followed the team across the water became veterans of European football in their own right, just like the team, an experienced professional army whose knowledge spanned the continent and spawned a thousand tales to tell and songs to sing, an unrivalled football folklore to be handed down to each successive generation, thirsting to experience what they had absorbed from their predecessors, from their fathers and uncles and elder brothers and just people from the pub, of exotic faraway places and exciting times. Witness the words of a song that emerged somewhere between winning that first European Cup in 1977 and the following year's successful defence of the trophy at Wembley; to the tune of 'Lili Marlene':

'Underneath the floodlights out in Dusseldorf
All the Kop were singing
Bevvied up of course
We've been to Lisbon and to Rome
And our team never walks alone
We're going back to Wembley
To win the Cup at home'

Wherever Liverpool played, from Milan to Moscow, Sofia to Kiev, you could overhear fans arranging to meet in a certain bar at a certain time, as matter-of-factly as if they were talking about meeting in a pub in Liverpool. These seen-it-all, done-it-all supporters from that proud city felt they were an elite, a category apart from the inexperienced, inexpert and very occasional foreign ramblings of the fans of other English clubs. They were the regulars. They would taunt their rivals with: 'Do you know where Europe is?' and offer to draw them maps.

They also felt apart from the poor reputation of English fans and in particular fans of the England national team, apart from the abusive, drunken, violent, hate-filled, racist, xenophobic stereotype, from seeking to be an all-conquering army of occupation. They regarded themselves as the exception, a category apart, a bit more savvy, more interested in integrating with locals rather than subjugating and intimidating them.

To illustrate the point, here's British football's record of football violence that preceded Heysel:

1972, Glasgow Rangers suspended from European football

for two years after fans rioted when in Barcelona for a match against Moscow Dynamo.

1974, Tottenham barred from playing their next two European matches at White Hart Lane after fans rioted during their UEFA Cup Final second leg tie in Rotterdam.

1977, Manchester United withdrawn from the European Cup Winners Cup after crowd trouble in St Etienne, France. Later reinstated but ordered to play home ties at least 125 miles from Manchester.

1980, England fined after fans rioted in Turin during European Championship match against Belgium. West Ham fined and ordered to play next two European home matches at least 187 miles from London after their fans rioted in Madrid during a European Cup Winners Cup match against Castilla. Fine subsequently lifted, return tie against Castilla played behind closed doors.

1981, English fans cause £60,000 worth of damage by rioting in Basle after a World Cup defeat by Switzerland.

1982, Aston Villa fans riot during European Cup match against Anderlecht.

1984, 200 British soccer fans held in Brussels after bloody riot.

Liverpool were involved in European football for every single one of those years, reaching six finals, which meant they actually played even more games. Their name does not appear once in that 'list of shame'.

That's not to claim that Liverpool FC is or was ever followed solely by angels. Liverpool fans are as capable of noisy, anti-social behaviour as any others, and certainly there are many who regard anything less than stupefying inebriation as a missed opportunity. They are probably market leaders in petty theft, scallying and 'bunking', the subtle black art of not paying for things. The difference was that they rarely went looking for trouble in Europe. The vandalism so often associated with England's supporters was never part of the Liverpool repertoire. No burning of national flags, no disrespecting local customs, nothing more than a bit of banter and piss-taking. There was a line not to be crossed — steal it maybe, but don't wreck it. If anything, Liverpool supporters seem to take pride in mingling into a place and talking to its people, trying to win them over. Better to have them with you than against you. After all, they're the ones serving your beer and your food, driving your taxi and running your accommodation. As a result, Liverpool's supporters have made many more friends than enemies during their frequent travels, gaining and earning trust from citizens who were prepared to give them the benefit of the doubt and offer a cautious welcome, despite the fearsome reputation of English football fans generally. The friendliness was usually reciprocated, and Liverpool's supporters developed a reputation as honourable exceptions to an ugly rule.

May 25th, 1977. A magic date for Liverpool supporters, captured in the Kop's version of 'Arrivederci Roma' — 'We're on our way to Roma, on the twenty fifth of May'. The day Liverpool became European Champions for the first time, the day the dream became reality and domestic supremacy was extended Europe-wide. The Liverpool legions — as many as 40,000 — descended upon the Eternal City to see Liverpool defeat the German team Borussia Monchengladbach.

I was one of many thousands unfortunate enough to travel on one of the special trains laid on for the match. More than twenty of them left Liverpool Lime Street station on the Monday afternoon for the game on Wednesday evening. A French railway strike meant the trains had to be re-routed through Belgium and Germany, and were not scheduled to arrive in Rome until early on Wednesday morning — a round trip of around seventy hours' worth of train travel. And this was emphatically not the Orient Express. If the duration of the journey was arduous enough, the condition of the trains was sub-human. Our train ran out of water by Tuesday lunchtime. Nobody could wash or, worse still, use the toilets. Passengers were forced to relieve themselves in plastic bags. No food or drink was available, so whenever the trains stopped at a station everyone had to jump off, use the toilets and buy what they could at station buffets. With over a thousand supporters on each train, the queues were instant and devastating.

The late spring heat in the trains was stifling and unrelenting throughout Tuesday, until nightfall brought some relief. With eight people crammed into compartments designed for six, any two at one time had to lie in the overhead luggage nets. The lack of respect and human dignity shown to the travellers — customers, we'd be called nowadays — was indicative of the way football fans were regarded; treated like cattle for live export, a commodity to be transported.

The condition of the huge trains that snaked into Rome Tiburtina station that Wednesday morning was, unsurprisingly, unspeakable. However the real wonder was not the extent of the mess and the stench, but rather that a thousand English football fans had not dismantled the wretched trains altogether and turned their attention to those who had treated them so badly and charged them extortionately for the privilege. When they finally emerged from this living hell, they did so with great good humour and dignity. Once loose on the streets of Rome, they admittedly produced a culture shock, and not only through sheer numbers. They blocked the traffic, swam in the fountains and were a nuisance to young women.

Stripped to the waist in the spring sunshine, many were noisy and drunk in the cafés, bars and piazzas. One Italian newspaper, *Repubblica*, claimed that at last Italians would be able to shed their inferiority complex about supposedly impeccable standards of British behaviour.

But when the same fans came to leave the city two days later, many to face that nightmare return train journey, opinions had shifted. *Il Messagero* wrote "What were all our fears about? There was no rape, no pillage. The horde passed by without violence, debauchery or depravity." (You can see the high standards that were expected of us.) "The only thing Roma can offer Liverpool is an apology plus well played, thanks and have a safe journey home."

The British press was equally complimentary. In its report on Liverpool's victory, *The Times* wrote: "Here there was nothing but friendly greetings, and all of football's problems seemed far away. It was later to become a night when British football could be proud of its champions and its followers." Even *The Sun*, still shunned and despised today by Liverpool supporters years after its grotesque post-Hillsborough coverage, carried a footnote reading: "In Rome newspapers praised the Liverpool fans for the way they behaved. A British Embassy spokesman said 'Everything went so smoothly.' Police in Liverpool said there had been only four arrests." The most penetrating observation appeared in *The Daily Mail*: "I hope that the best part of the legend Liverpool leave behind is that they proved you can have bacchanalia without going beyond the limits. My final memory is of a Liverpool fan of ferocious appearance and impressively drunk at the reception. He lurched over to the Minister of Sport, Denis Howell, and said 'Don't worry mister, we're going to have the time of our lives. But we're not Leeds or Man United. You will not be ashamed of us.'"

For eight more years he was right. Other successful European Cup Finals followed, in 1978 at Wembley and 1981 in Paris, where the team's 'lovely, lively, raucous fans' (Daily Mirror) travelled to see Liverpool play Real Madrid, amidst the strictest security I have ever witnessed at a football match. Outside the Parc des Princes Stadium, the infamous CRS riot police sat by the van-load, Gallic Darth Vaders in their black cloaks and helmets. They were not needed. After another Liverpool victory, amidst scenes of wild celebration in the French capital, a Paris police spokesman said, "It is pleasing to see how well everybody is behaving. There were so many real supporters that I think any bad element has been snuffed out." Once again, there were only a handful of arrests for drunk and disorderly behaviour, a few minor incidents to blot the record. Restraint had again prevailed.

May 1984 and we were back in Rome, scene of the club's finest hour seven years earlier. The legions dusted off their 'Emperors of Rome' T-shirts to relive the glory of '77. This time, however, the opposition represented the greatest potential threat yet to Liverpool's supporters' good reputation in Europe. It was Roma themselves. UEFA had decided to stick with the originally planned venue for the final despite Roma's appearance in it — an interesting interpretation of the idea of a neutral venue for the final. The Italian club's first-ever appearance in a major European final would take place on their own home ground in their own city. We were cast in the role of the demons, the bad guys out to spoil the party and slay the dragon in its own lair.

It didn't feel fair at the time, and still doesn't. With the passion and near-hysteria that surrounds Italian football, the biggest match in Roma's history would create a super-charged backdrop, and the potential for crowd trouble spilling over the sides of the bubbling seething cauldron was all too easy to foresee. We knew it, the police knew it, the football authorities should have known it, but refused to contemplate switching the venue.

Our group was amongst the advance guard of Liverpool supporters to arrive in Rome, in mid-afternoon the day before the game. As our train, a normal service one this time, not a football special (once bitten) slid through the grey drab outskirts, the bits you don't think of when you think of Rome, we saw a city ablaze with Roma's red and yellow colours, tower blocks festooned with Roma flags, draped over balconies, displayed in windows, fluttering from rooftops, and unforgettably, a monumental flag draped from the top of a tower block and covering much of one facade of it. How do you make a flag that big? On the streets, Roma flags flew from the open windows of horn-blowing Fiats and, balanced precariously on the pillions of a million motor scooters, unfeasibly large clusters of swarthy youths, three or four to a scooter, waved their flags, punched the air and shouted 'Forza Roma!' in wide-eyed excitement, the driver pumping the horn mercilessly. On every street corner, hastily erected stalls sold flags and colours and klaxons and all manner of Roma paraphernalia, the red and yellow fluttering in the bright sunlight. And with still over twenty-four hours to go, it wasn't even match day yet! The match had the city firmly in its grip; its very air tingled with the anticipation. It felt like a city on the brink. Just light the blue touch paper and stand back.

Yet, as we sat drinking in the city centre's American Bar that Tuesday evening, for all the world like a bunch of tourists, the contrast between the scare stories and vivid headlines in the UK newspapers ('Roman Wall' and 'City of Fear', accompanied by grim photos of phalanxes of riot police) could not have been more stark. Whilst families and friends at home were being whipped into apprehension on our behalf, a glance at the Italian newspapers told a very different story; one of escalating British violence during the miners' strike. Later that evening there would be a few minor skirmishes between Romans and Liverpool supporters in the streets near the Trevi Fountain, but the tension never spilled over into the predicted large-scale confrontations.

The spectacle awaiting us on match day inside the Olympic Stadium was overwhelming. 12,000 Liverpool supporters were lost amidst a flag-waving, horn-blowing tumult of 50,000 fanatical Italians mounting an assault of sound and vision. Fire-crackers, smoke bombs and searing red flares, huge flags gradually being unfurled to cover entire sections of crowd, klaxons and thunderous chanting and singing, an insane cacophony. It will stay in our minds forever. The odds seemed insurmountable. You could almost have forgiven the Liverpool players for refusing to leave the sanctity and sanity of their dressing room. "It must have been like this at the Colosseum", muttered someone behind. "The Christians got an away win though didn't they?" The sight that greeted — if greeted is the appropriate term- the Liverpool players as they walked from the tunnel must have made even players of their vast experience quake. A cascade of rockets exploded into the sky releasing clouds of red and yellow smoke, an almost unbroken bank of Roma banners waved, the noise deafened, with the Italians in almost hysterical fever pitch. But amongst Liverpool's fans a very British defiance in adversity kicked in, and the 12,000 sang and shouted themselves to a standstill in an effort to lift their team and counter the overwhelming odds.

History shows that we went and antagonised the hordes by winning, and in the most antagonising way possible at that, through sudden death penalties. 'Sudden death' seemed a disturbingly portentous term to describe the fate awaiting us outside the ground afterwards. Predictably, given that we'd just beaten the home team on penalties in their biggest ever match, there was mayhem. As the Liverpool supporters stayed inside the ground to witness the presentation of that mighty trophy to their club for a fourth time and the lap of honour, the Italian fans vanished, emptying over three-quarters of the stadium in what seemed like seconds. We guessed where a fair proportion of them might be. Sure enough, when the time came to take a deep breath and find our way back to the city centre, the pandemonium began. Sounds of shouting and sirens and howling dogs carried towards us on the still night air, from what seemed like every direction, a psychological onslaught before the physical one began. Groups of Liverpool fans kept returning to the ground with tales of roads being too dangerous to pass along. Most decided to wait anxiously for a while to see if the trouble died down a bit and whether the police would be successful in clearing a way through the Italian fans and keeping them at bay. Our coach, when it finally came, was attacked and hit repeatedly by bricks, stones and bottles as it came to cross the river Tiber back to the city centre. Several windows were cracked and two exploded inwards, showering glass over us. The city centre was unnaturally, eerily quiet, as if under curfew, and very tense. Rome was not going to be the easiest place to celebrate. All the bars we tried were closed to us — except one. The owner of one small back street café bar was more than happy to welcome us, because, as he proudly proclaimed, he was a Juventus supporter, and as such a friend of anyone who defeated the detested Roma. You can only speculate how much his feelings towards us had changed twelve months later.

What trouble there had been in Rome was instigated

mostly by the host city's supporters, and once again, Liverpool's supporters emerged with some credit, from police, press and locals alike. However, it could be argued that the seeds of the Heysel tragedy were really sowed in Rome. Tales abounded of roaming scooter gangs hunting down Liverpool supporters, stabbing and slashing dozens, including one 13-year-old boy who needed 200 stitches in his face. There was little protection from the police, who routinely attacked and robbed English supporters in revenge for the defeat of the local team. Before the match, it was alleged that stewards and gate attendants had taken watches, cameras and items of jewellery from visiting supporters. That night, many desperate English fans, deserted by Italian coach drivers booked to drive them to Rome airport, sought sanctuary at the British Embassy. And many may have thought there was a score to settle against — well, any Italians.

The reason for this foray into Liverpool supporters' European history is that if, prior to Heysel, they were tarred with the general English football hooligan brush, then they did not deserve to be. Despite the number of games Liverpool had played in Europe, despite the violent prevailing terrace culture in England, Liverpool supporters had no particular reputation for violence, outside of an intense rivalry with Manchester United. There had been no major crowd trouble, no mass rioting, no TV and press headlines, no footage of the sort of brawling so often seen with England fans abroad. It incensed us to be bracketed with them. We had no form, no previous, just a relatively clean record of twenty years' good-ish behaviour.

John Williams of the Sir Norman Chester Centre for Football Research at Leicester University, a Liverpool supporter, summed it up like this: "Liverpool terrace culture was at odds with the kind of hooliganism that blighted the game from the mid-Seventies onwards. There were often fights at matches, but in general Liverpool fans were not really interested in violence, although they could look after themselves. The idea of being a 'scally' was to be above the kind of pointless destruction which neanderthals like Leeds or Chelsea or England fans went in for. That is why Liverpool fans were never organised into firms; there were just small bunches of mates who stood together at the match or in the pub. It was okay to steal — as long as what you stole was designer stuff from Europe or wherever. It was just funny stuff, larking about."

According to David Lacey in *The Guardian*, "Heysel was the first time in 21 years of competition that Liverpool has been involved in serious violence."

Anybody who knew the culture of Liverpool FC and its supporters at that time knew that something rang false in all the media accounts. *Heysel was and still is totally alien to Liverpool football culture.*

So when the Popplewell Report on crowd safety at football matches, commissioned by the UK Government in the wake of Heysel, stated: "It was unbelievable that the Belgian authorities had been told, by football authorities and the English police, that the English fans would cause little or no trouble. That had a marked effect on precautions", it missed the point. Based on Liverpool's history, rather than England's or English clubs' generally, the advice to the Belgians from across the Channel had been entirely reasonable, and based on precedent. Those English football authorities and English police knew their football better than Judge Popplewell, who, in common with many in the media and the wider public, failed to make the distinction between the crowd records and reputations of Liverpool's supporters and English fans generally. Because until Heysel, there was a distinction, one that meant a lot to us and was something worth preserving.

After all, why should there be anything different in the club's 140th European game from the previous 139?

CHAPTER 3
AND SO TO BELGIUM

As the end of May drew closer, the anticipation and excitement grew. Those few special, precious days that lay ahead became the all-consuming focus of our entire existences, etched in glorious technicolour against the monochrome monotony of working life and domestic routine. There was nothing else before them or beyond them. For those few exotic, exhilarating days, we knew we would be living on our own terms and our own wits, semi-feral, relying solely on ourselves and each other, freed from the shackles of convention, expectation and responsibility. The game of football is just the event at the core of a much wider experience, bundled up with companionship, shared experience and mutual reliance. It's the travelling, the adventure and the freedom, an intoxicating concoction of pleasure and duty, a melange of military manoeuvre and religious crusade, and we would savour every drop. Because beyond it, when it was all behind us, win or lose, crashing anti-climax awaited.

Monday, May 27th, 1985.

Excited like a child waiting for Santa, I awoke far too early. Outside, the streets of my home town were getting their early morning spruce-up in preparation for the annual Whit Monday parade and carnival. Today it seemed even more parochial and trivial than ever, only reinforcing the epic scale of our grand European adventure. We had far bigger fish to fry.

I checked my packing: some changes of clothes and personal effects, some food and lots of beer for the travelling. It is a matter of some misplaced macho pride amongst young British males to see who has brought the largest, and therefore funniest, amount of alcohol with him. Being sensible, I had also packed bottled water and a carton of fruit juice, tucked almost apologetically into the dark, distant recesses of my holdall. Also, with slightly anally retentive foresight, I'd packed a form of breakfast for Tuesday morning (well they don't have food in Belgium do they?). We were due to arrive in Ostend at about 6am the following morning, after 18 hours of continuous travelling, a day and night of almost unbroken beer drinking and little or no sleep. For some reason I had decided a hard-boiled egg, bread and butter and fruit juice, probably eaten on the move in the early morning streets, would be just what I wanted at that time.

Six of us met at lunchtime: my co-prize winner Vince, Phil, Alan, John and Mark, a Birkenhead-born exile living in the Midlands. Judging by appearances would give entirely the wrong impression of Mark; despite the intimidating tattoos, ear stud and punky spiked carrot top hair, Mark is in fact friendliness incarnate, and will chatter incessantly about more or less anything. His only enemy seems to be silence. The other two, Don and Trisha (a married couple), would meet us in London later. Don had already suffered weeks of abuse about taking his wife to the match; it must have been the only way he could get his pass-out.

Half a dozen bulging, misshapen, clanking holdalls confirmed that everyone had risen to the beer cans challenge. As we passed through Birmingham New Street station, I regarded the scurrying commuters and aimless loafers with a sense of utter supremacy. In startling contrast to my customary Monday morning auto-pilot, I felt deliciously alive and tingling with purpose. This Monday morning I would swap places with absolutely nobody.

A matter of minutes into the journey and the first tell-tale metallic rip, hiss of escaping air and inevitable jet of beer spray up the train window declared proceedings officially open. John grinned sheepishly. The journey to London lightened the holdalls considerably.

We met up with Don and Trisha at Victoria, and went to catch the train to Dover. A number of Liverpool supporters, including some we knew or recognised, were already loitering around the station concourse, and we exchanged idle chat about tickets, where they were staying — the usual stuff. This advance guard was the campaign-hardened hardcore, supporters who would always make their own way, scornfully disdainful of the organised trips. In stark contrast to the flag- and scarf-bedecked, replica shirt-wearing day-trippers who would follow later in their hordes, these were a riot of anonymity, conspicuous only for their lack of team identification, save maybe for the occasional small LFC metal lapel badge. To them, wearing team colours is just plain naff, a wholly unnecessary way of demonstrating your allegiance, just pandering to commercial interests and the authorities' desire to know who you were, which makes you easier to control. They were Reds and didn't care whether the world knew it or not. The important ones knew. The team would know, when it was time. The rest did not matter. You wouldn't have known these were Liverpool supporters, or even football supporters at all, unless you heard the accents and worked it out.

At this point, a familiar phenomenon struck, and with a depressing inevitability it concerned Vince. Exchanging currency is yet another area of life with which Vince does not mesh. He is to foreign currency transactions as the moth to the light bulb. He just can't resist them. We recalled how, the year before in Rome, he had taken with him a little-known brand of Eurocheques that nobody had ever heard of. In order to demonstrate their crushing superiority over our own dull mainstream means, it had been necessary for him to visit every bank he passed, about every two hours, whilst the rest of us struggled by with just one single visit to cover the whole three days.

Instantly, the exchange bureau/bureau de change/cambio/ Wechsel at Victoria had Vince in its spell. Everyone knows these bureaux do not offer the best exchange rates, but it was too late. Its siren counter called. As Vince was the only one of us who didn't already possess any Belgian currency, we had to acknowledge that at some point he did need some. Otherwise he'd be trying to borrow off us all the time. Within what seemed like seconds, Vince, ever the master of non-verbal communication, had become embroiled in some kind of haggling, hand-waving and wild gesticulating. There he remained, wildly gesticulating. For twenty minutes. What is there to get into debate about exactly?

"I'd like some Belgian currency please."

"Certainly sir, how much?"

The current exchange rates are displayed. You wait a few seconds, accept the wad, say "thank you" and leave. Where is the scope within that for discussion and conflict? Vince, however, has the rare gift of perceiving danger where others cannot. I suspect it was at the root of the demolition of his relationship with his travel agent and the tragic demise of our free holiday. His rip-off sensors must have been flashing today too, and whenever they do, his world becomes a different and dark place. Even the most straightforward of propositions become logistical minefields. A relatively complex transaction such as changing currency can quickly become a spectator sport, and we duly spectated, arms folded and with gathering incredulity, before he finally reappeared, clutching his currency and explaining what had happened in minute detail that nobody even pretended to listen to. "You're a fucking mong Vince" was Don's harsh but fair summary.

As we clambered and clanked on board the train for Dover, we saw, just a few seats further down the carriage, the unmistakeable figure of another Liverpool supporter we all knew very well indeed. We knew what to expect. He was a bearded Brummie who possesses one real talent in life. Not one that lends itself to career prospects, admittedly, but undeniably a skill of sorts. He communicates almost exclusively in profanities. No innocent word above one syllable is ever safe from violation, from having its middle regions defiled by an affront to public decency or a bestial act inserted either before or after it. He was — is — spectacularly brilliant at it. Marriage, fatherhood, the passing of time, none has dimmed his light. His astounding, encyclopaedic command of obscenities has reached the point of street art, like verbal graffiti. The Expletive Variations. He could have compiled a Profanosaurus years before Viz came up with theirs. As part of his armoury he has clear, black-and-white views on just about everything and grey areas about nothing. He is also one of the club's most loyal supporters, having barely missed a game, home or away, since the early 1970s.

To the acute embarrassment of ourselves and all innocent rail travellers within five times normal earshot, he spotted us and greeted us in his unique vernacular: "Fuckin' 'ell, it's the wankers. You're a wanker, you're a wanker, ..." (He went through each of us in turn, pointing to each so as to avoid confusion as to which one of us was a wanker. As it turned out, we all were.) "Liverpool are playin' in red you know. Roger Hunt's packed up you know. Fuckin' part-timers. Got your scarves, your little European Cup Final hats? Managed to book a ferry? Couldn't run a fuckin' bath ...". This was his version of 'hello'. The trick, we knew, was to weather the initial storm, absorb the buffeting and let its fire blow out — just the way Liverpool had learned to play in Europe really. Dampen the crowd's ardour, kill its ability to inspire its own team, then set about beating them.

After the initial onslaught had indeed blown itself out, we asked him what he thought about the forthcoming match. Surprisingly enough, all the Italians turned out to be wankers as well, and, not being one to overlook a nationalistic stereotype, one hard tackle and they wouldn't want to know, they'll be screaming and whining and rolling over on the grass — sorry, fuckin' grass — and so on. We asked how his life was going generally, and received a response that was a classic even by his high standards. He managed to engineer room in the two syllables of his employer's name for an expletive. 'Where you workin' these days then?' 'Peu-fuckin'–geot.' I've never forgotten Peu-fuckin'–geot; I have to stop myself sometimes to realise that it isn't the actual name of that well-known French car manufacturer. But he had been off for a week with a new disease called derma-bastard–titis.

On a train, or in any confined space, typical reactions to a group of football fans, particularly one with the Brummie's peculiar grasp of language, might include fear, caution, revulsion, a kind of panicky over-compensatory friendliness and the self-preservatory need to appear as one with their boorishness, or a simmering, smouldering indignation and resentment at this usurping of a legitimate journey. But in our midst, hitherto unknown to us, was a fellow passenger who fell into another category entirely. He was an archetypal professional Yorkshireman, the sort who's proud to be blunt, calls a spade a spade, and so on. (Incidentally, why is calling a spade a spade anything to be proud of? Anyone can do it, it's easy. 'Oh look, there's a spade.' There, see? *Easy*.)

This particular sample of the species was middle-aged, balding down the middle, short and stocky, and, as we were about to discover, very opinionated in an affable large-slobbery-dog-jumping-up-to-lick-your-face sort of way. He was also more than willing to enter a spot of verbal jousting with any other bigot who appeared on his radar, like our Brummie mate. Next to him sat a mousy near-mute of a wife who presumably knew her place and was probably (and understandably) petrified of the situation, and of what her husband might do or say next. But her warrior husband clearly perceived no danger in taking on a dozen football fans and a torrent of vitriol in a confined train carriage. All he saw was an opportunity to gain a new audience. With his volume set to eleven, he gatecrashed our conversation the very moment he heard one of us loudly and colourfully denouncing a can of beer as being — well, something that ended with 'southern piss'. It was just the opening Yorkie craved. "You're bloody reet theer. It's roobish, is southern beer. Shall ah tell thee wheer't best beer comes from? Yorkshire!" he said triumphantly, as proud at knowing this secret as if he'd just discovered how to turn base metal into gold.

"Ah'm from Yorkshire me sen, near Donny. I'm goin' on 'oliday joost nah." (I expect he meant "we", unless his wife was just escorting him as far as Dover, which come to think of it wasn't such an outlandish idea.)

"It's called Stones," he continued. "Stones Bitter. T'strongest pint in England, and 't'best." He sat back and crossed his arms, proud of his forthrightness, his interestingness, of Stones beer, of knowing of Stones beer, of coming from the same county as Stones beer, oh just of his sheer bloody Yorkshireness.

Now I'm all for regional dialects, I observe them keenly and relish the diversity they bring, although the South Yorkshire one does seem to make life unnecessarily hard; what with all those stuttering 't's and sudden abrupt glottal stops, it's like when one of your speakers is intermittently on the blink. I also take an interest in my beer, real ale and all that. And I also find that if there is anything more irritating than someone being smug, it's someone being smug about being hopelessly wrong. So I tossed in a verbal hand grenade, waited three seconds and pulled the pin: "That's bollocks mate, it's not even the strongest in Yorkshire. Or t'best. What about Taylor's Landlord then?"

The grenade was not a dud. Swivelling round, eyes bulging and ablaze, temples throbbing with indignation, he rounded on me, unable to remain seated. "Roobish! Bloody roobish! Reet, yo', yo' and all't rest a yo buggers, I'll take t'lot a yer to me social club in Donny reet nah and pour a gallon a Stones down thee. Ah can guarantee yo'll not be able to walk aht agin!"

Oh well, point proved then. Game, set and match. His meek wife gave a little tug on his shirt sleeve. "Sit down George" she said, meekly. "You'll have a coronary."

"Yeah sit down George, do as yer fuckin' told, yer Yorkshire twat", added guess-who, helpfully.

"Nah, theer alreet duck, theer joost tryin' to wind me oop! Theer me mates these."

Mates? We'd hardly even been introduced! But you had to admire George's spirit — undaunted, unbowed, un-intimidated, irrepressible. We told him we were on our way to the match in Brussels, he wished us luck — he always wanted English teams to do well of course, except Manchester United — 'can't bloody abide them'. That elevated him immediately in our estimation. We left him alone to contemplate his wife and a week without Stones Bitter.

The train snaked on through the East London sprawl, drawing the odd V-sign — not the victory one — from some local youth who realised who we were and where we were going, and we duly reciprocated, throwing in the odd 'wanker' gesture just for variation. Food, cigarettes and more beer saw us through to Dover. Canned beer, although universally foul in my estimation, is better than none, and had done its job. It was 7.30pm, with the ferry not due till after midnight. The job of keeping us sedated would now pass to the pubs of Dover.

Bodies spilled out onto the platform, closely followed by holdalls and empty cans and food wrappers. One or two wandered off in search of a chip shop, the rest opted for the pub nearest the station. Our ferry was from Eastern Dock, the opposite end of town, so a pub crawl was unavoidable even if we didn't fancy one. A farcical pool knockout got underway without ever really developing. Glancing outside, I noticed the weather was deteriorating suddenly and drastically. The blue skies of a fine spring evening had morphed appreciably into a threatening heavy grey, and a wind had sprung up that was already bending trees over. (It's the sort of thing I notice because I am no mariner, doubtless a source of huge private disappointment to my ex-Navy father. Speaking as the only human I've ever known to part company with his breakfast on the 20-minute ferry crossing to the Isle of Mull, I viewed the change in conditions with abject misery. Only those who get seasick will understand. The others, who don't, basically didn't give a toss.)

As we left the pub for the trek across town, the daylight beginning to fade and Dover's lights beginning to twinkle, my spirits began to sag. Out to sea, a fog had descended, part-mist, part-drizzle, draping the world beyond the lighthouse and the harbour wall in an impenetrable ghostly grey shroud. The wind had died almost as quickly as it had sprung into life, leaving an unnerving stillness. Visibility was down to a few hundred yards and falling. Soon even the lighthouse disappeared; only its light dimly remained. The fog held the sea in its grip. From somewhere beyond the grey curtain came the mournful, muffled boom of the fog siren, that menacing harbinger of maritime disaster. The scene was curiously disquieting. As another desolate, unearthly boom echoed across the harbour, the cheery lights of the next pub offered an inviting respite from creeping despondency. Last port of call before Dover Eastern Docks was a pub called the Albion. I wonder whether it's still there, or whether it's now a passing whim theme pub or overpriced private flats ....

Those who had not visited the chippy ordered food, or in one instance claimed and ate somebody else's; they were just arguing with the waitress about where their food was, they'd been waiting half an hour ("honestly, I brought your order, those over there said it was theirs ...".) But "those over there" had already left and merged into the night. I made do with a surreptitiously swallowed seasick pill, which is low on credibility amongst fellow football fans but good news for any passenger within five yards of me during the crossing. At around midnight, we struggled bleary-eyed and moderately pissed into the docks, only to hear an announcement that the sailing would be delayed by approximately one hour because of the fog. Better news was the relatively small number of fellow passengers we had to share the boat with. In a zombie trance of travel tiredness, with eleven hours of almost continual drinking and the beginning of the travel pill's effects, I fetched an abysmal coffee in a plastic cup from a vending machine and telephoned home to confirm that we were as yet unscathed, to the inevitable and depressingly predictable chorus of: "I just called to say I love you". Before long we were all crashed out semi-conscious and dozing on the benches beneath the humming strip lights of the waiting room. Is it not possible to run them off dimmer switches at night and in the early hours? Sweaty, sticky, clammy, gritty-eyed, I tried to catch some sleep. Such periodic lows are of course an integral part of these low-budget endurance tests.

Somewhere out there a fog-bound ferry, the one we had to catch for its return journey, was trying to find its way across the English Channel and into harbour. Finally the announcement came; could we now move to the dockside to prepare to embark. After the warmth and stuffiness of the waiting room, the chill of the night air was welcome, invigorating and reviving. But the sight that awaited us as we turned the corner to join the queue was enough to jolt a corpse into life. At the far end of the jetty, facing the foot passengers, was a gang of maybe 50 motorbikers, all denim and swastika'd leathers, chains and Viking helmets, headlights blazing straight towards us, silhouetted against the dark, meanness oozing from every pore. It looked like a film set. The word 'Stuttgart' was emblazoned across many of the jackets, helmets or gothic buckle belts. They could have been making a Motorhead video.

So here were hundreds of English football fans, most in an advanced state of alcoholic disrepair, about to share a cross-channel ferry with a gang of German bikers. Anyone spot the potential for trouble? We could see the headlines already. The passengers who belonged to neither camp just looked miserable, trying to position themselves as far from the bikers and football fans as possible without falling into the sea. You had to feel sorry for them. But cometh the hour, cometh the scouser. A lone Liverpool supporter, seemingly oblivious to the dynamics of the situation, sauntered nonchalantly towards the massed bikers, munching a bag of crisps. He laid his hand on one of the sacred bikes, a 1,000cc monster with another on its back, and, calmly enquired in broadest scouse: "Gizza go on yer scooter there lad."

After a supercharged silence and a collective holding of breath, the belittled biker smiled a thin, watery smile and said in German English: "You want to sit on my bike? Sure!" and jumped off. The spell was broken. Within seconds the bikers were infiltrated by dozens of curious football fans, prodding and jabbing, asking infernal questions about the bikes and their owners and where they had been. Just being friendly, really. The bikers just sat on their bikes and tolerated it, looking mildly bewildered and smiling self-consciously. It reminded me of those wildlife films in which a much larger body is overwhelmed by an army of ants. An international incident was thus averted, the culture chasm separating German bikers and English football fans amicably bridged. A small victory for the human race.

Just think, tonight and every night as you lie asleep in your bed, a scene like this could be unfolding somewhere in these isles....

The only parts of a ferry that football fans know exists

are the duty free and the bar, and that's where we gathered, maybe 200 in all. Plus our 50 German biker friends. Bars on ferries normally close when football fans are expected in any numbers, but who'd expect them on this early hours crossing, more than 40 hours before the game? The bar was open. I felt I'd already had sufficient beer for now, besides it doesn't go well with seasick pills. With the travelling and the beer and the seasick pills, I crashed out across some bench seats in a semi-conscious stupor, only dimly aware of the incessant banter and continued drinking, growing more raucous and animated with each pint. The enthusiasm for the task in hand had no upper limit, the capacity and endurance defying explanation. There is peer pressure of course, of not wanting to show weakness by missing a round at the bar, not wanting to admit defeat by falling asleep. A robotic, distinctly unmusical singing began, usually performed from a slumped, near-horizontal position, heads lolling back and forth, glasses slopping over floor or clothing, lyrics dredged from somewhere deep within the memory banks. Fragments of a song here, a half-finished anthem there, usually at the wrong speed and in the wrong key, but hey, we're on our way to the European Cup Final so who cares?

I slumbered fitfully through the discord, drifting in and out of consciousness. You never really sleep in those circumstances. Through a space someone had cleared in the condensation on a porthole, I could see the blackness of the sea at night just beginning to give way to the first pale grey light of morning, a thin line along the horizon. The fog had lifted — outside at any rate — and I could just make out the dim outline of the Belgian coast, lights twinkling. It's curious how the sight of land seems to rejuvenate mind and body.

As I came around, my mouth felt like (in the immortal words of Blackadder) there'd been a Frenchman living in it. It seemed that we may have another problem too. Whilst I'd been crashed out, John and Vince had treated themselves to a bottle or two of Pernod from the duty-free. Barely an inch remained in the bottom, sloshing around as the boat entered choppier coastal waters. The bottle was in the tentative grip of a comatose John. But Vince, my room-mate-to-be in an hour or so, was marginally worse — utterly, irretrievably paralytic, beyond assistance and beyond reason. Vince and John's Pernod predilection had surfaced a year earlier, on a French train on our way to Rome, when John continued to drink from a broken glass, his mouth heading unerringly towards the cut part every time.

It was easy, even through the mental smog, to appreciate the potential gravity of this situation. It's not as if we hadn't discussed it. Before and after major football matches on the continent, security is at its highest. We all knew every ferry arriving from England would be under suspicion and close scrutiny. Anyone even suspected of being a football fan ran the risk of being detained, charged or sent straight back home on the slightest pretext. Or batoned into oblivion in the nearest cell. (Which wouldn't have made Vince any worse.) Even 36 hours before the match, we knew there would be a significant police presence at Ostend docks, and we didn't want this to be the nearest we got to the European Cup Final. We had talked about making a low-key, uneventful arrival and disembarkation, then just melting away into the streets, finding our accommodation, checking in, getting a few hours' sleep and meeting later. Instead we had two barely-conscious human-shaped Pernod holders capable neither of standing up nor the other prerequisite, shutting up. If their condition was noticed — and it was hard to see how it wouldn't be — there was a good possibility we'd be on the next ferry back to England, or spending some unwelcome time in an Ostend police cell. Phil was furiously unimpressed, seeing it as totally unprofessional behaviour. He too can have his moments, but perhaps picks them better than this. "We don't need this, I'm not going to be happy if we miss everything because of these pissed-up twats." Pot and kettle sprang to mind. He suggested we try to wedge them between us and walk down the exit. The world's first Siamese quadruplets. It might at least prevent them from lurching uncontrollably into innocent civilians or the sea, and catching the eye of the watching, waiting police. It wasn't as if the rest of us were fresh as daisies ourselves. Just don't give them any reason to take an interest, that's the golden rule that we were now in danger of breaking.

As the ferry shuddered to a halt, on 'B' deck there was feverish activity verging on panic. Even fumbling for documentation could be enough to attract unwanted attention, so we faced the unenviable task of rummaging through holdalls full of crushed empty beer cans with razor-edged ring pull holes, left-over sandwiches, sticky melted chocolate wrappers and God knows what else to find John's and Vince's passports and ferry tickets.

The fact that such an assembly can pass through passport control, customs and 'rigid police scrutiny' without being challenged was — shall we kindly say? — a testimony to the *laissez faire* nature of the Belgians, something we would see much more of later. So with two lifeless corpses wedged between us, the eight of us entered the continent of Europe. The first European 16-legged race? A few Liverpool fans that knew us spotted us and our predicament (not difficult), laughed and wished us luck. They told us they were heading for Blankenberge, a holiday resort a few miles up the coast. Phil muttered darkly to an inanely grinning, uncomprehending Vince that if he heard as much as a peep from him he'd lift him over that railing and drop the little bastard in the harbour.

Shortly before 6am, on what was already an achingly bright sunny May morning, we struggled onto the still-quiet streets of Ostend with our Pernod-stricken burden. Somewhere, an unsuspecting Hotel Pacific awaited two English holiday-makers under the name of Vince Bennett. Mr Bennett was barely able to walk or speak.

CHAPTER 4
MEN ARRIVING BADLY

Looking back, perhaps the single most valuable aspect of our free holiday turned out to be the complimentary Ostend street map. It told us that the Hotel Pacific might be fairly close to the docks in normal circumstances, although these were not those, as we battled like salmon up a weir, our 25% reduction in effective manpower making every 50 yards a labour. The handful of early morning Flems — if that's not too unpleasant a phrase to conjure with — going about their business didn't seem to know quite what to make of this bedraggled procession and its staggering, swaying, Pernod-afflicted tail. It was as if the circus freak show had come to town and was having a very early morning rehearsal.

John wasn't great, but it was Vince who stole the show. His facial expression had become a frankly disturbing hybrid of extra-terrestrial characters from both big and small screen — we variously thought ET, Yoda from Star Wars and, for those old enough, Zoony from Fireball XL5. His painfully deliberate sloth-like movements, punctuated by random outbreaks of uncontrolled staccato sideways steps as if attempting a dainty dressage, were accompanied by periodic twisted, distorted grins that broke and spread haphazardly across his features. Maybe he was just thrilled at his sheer brilliance in managing to remain upright-ish.

Don, now translating, interpreted a series of grunts and a seamless row of vowels as meaning that Yoda now felt sufficiently recovered to carry his own bags, a request that we were more than willing to concur with. He was pretty adamant about it too, groping through fresh air at those magical holdall straps and missing by only a matter of yards. Don made the decision to give him his bag to carry, with the charitable sentiment: 'Here you are then you little twat, I'll give it ten seconds before you fall over.' Vince stood there holding and cuddling his bag as though he really, really loved it, swaying precariously. He got underway again ... two slow, deliberate steps forward, five rapid involuntary ones sideways, regroup, forward again. But it wasn't long before the redistribution of weight created by the holdall proved too much for his highly delicate equilibrium. Without needing to look back, we knew exactly what had caused the loud metallic crash behind us, but we were half apprehensive and half amused to know how. The sight that greeted us will live on forever, all tiredness and irritation briefly banished in one glorious vision; a hapless sprawling Gollum-esque figure lying on its back on the pavement, covered in potato peel, fish bones, empty cartons and all the other nameless horrors you might expect to find in the average Belgian dustbin. Yet somehow it still clung tenaciously to its holdall straps, a deep bond now formed, and still wore that same inane grin, as though this was all a deliberate and hugely amusing part of its master plan. What else was there to do but laugh out loud and yell insults down the street?

Curtains twitched, windows opened, delivery men and market traders tut-tutted, the respectable burghers of an apprehensive town glanced at watches and shook their heads at seeing their worst fears confirmed. Oh God, they're here already. Fortunately, no police though. And so in this way, our elaborate plans for a quiet, low-key, unobtrusive, win-over-the-locals type of entry into Belgium were laid to rest. If, as an English football fan travelling soon before a high-profile match, you desire to find accommodation, bars and restaurants that will happily serve you, if you'd prefer to remain unacquainted with the local gendarmerie, a good way to ensure you fail utterly is to follow this example.

A journey of less than one mile to the hotel took an hour, and featured another near-disaster involving — well, Vince of course, as he suddenly surged uncontrollably and quite quickly forwards, straight towards the dropped tailgate of a delivery lorry, right at forehead height. Warnings stuck in throats, and we could only watch in horror as he avoided decapitation only with a last second duck, passing straight beneath the tailgate with a millimetre clearance, bent double Groucho Marx style (except Vince bent double isn't very tall at all — think chihuahua) whilst the driver watched on in bewilderment. Perhaps he didn't have drunks playing chicken with his tailgate before 7am most Tuesday mornings.

We finally found the Hotel Pacific, propped the two stupefied grinning casualties up against its wall and held a quick conference. The others decided to split into twos —

Phil and Mark, John and Alan, Don and Trisha — to improve the chances of finding rooms, as finding any place that could or would take all eight of us would be nigh on impossible. We arranged to meet later, at 5pm at the main railway station. Vince and I were left to our prize, the Hotel Pacific, whose understanding of our booking arrangements would only coincide with ours if a small miracle had occurred. Besides, the person who actually made all the arrangements, in whose name the booking was made, who would have been expected to be the one who knew exactly what had been booked in his name and deal with any queries arising, was slumped against the hotel's exterior wall and of zero use to himself, me or the hotel. Would our room be free yet? After all, 7.30am is quite early to check in for an evening. I sensed that the conversation I was about to have would be tricky even in my own language. I took a deep breath and entered the hotel alone.

The reception looked dingy after the piercing early morning light outside, and smelt a touch fusty, but by usual football standards it was reasonably impressive, even having its own reception area, in which sat an elderly night porter, peering at a newspaper in a booth illuminated by a bare light bulb. He glanced up over his spectacles and said, in heavily accented English: "Good morning, can I help you? Are you utterly clueless and shambolically drunk?" No, he didn't say the last bit, but he might as well have. How did he know I was English, given that I hadn't spoken yet? Don't Belgians, Dutch, Germans and others look very similar? Does Englishness just exude from every pore? Or had he just assumed that no other nationality could possibly be in this state so early in the morning?

I decided the easiest course of action would be to introduce myself as Mr Bennett, since the real one was slumped comatose against the outside wall. It might avoid having to make the sort of complicated explanation that I was so very ill-equipped to deal with. I cleared my throat and explained that my name was Bennett, I had a twin room booked for that evening and I had a travelling companion outside who was 'tired and unwell after much travelling and seasickness'. "Too many pills," I explained, making a wave motion with my hands, the best sea impression I could muster. To my surprise, the porter nodded sympathetically, looked down at some sort of register and handed me the key to a room. To my genuine surprise and relief, we were actually on the hotel's radar. Vince had at least got that bit right. First hurdle safely negotiated. I had hoped I wouldn't have to provide a resumé of the free holiday saga, as I didn't really understand it anyway. All I had to do now was to get Vince from his horizontal position on the pavement up to his room without attracting too much attention. Some task. We three-legged into reception, him still barely conscious, almost taking the door off its hinges in the process. Mercifully the porter had disappeared. I bundled my burden into the lift, bumping and thudding and bouncing off its metallic inner walls as we went. I looked up — straight into the anxious face of the porter, who unfortunately had returned. I had grown so accustomed to Vince's condition, I had completely forgotten the impact it might have on strangers.

"I told you he wasn't very well," I explained sheepishly. The porter said nothing, but probably spotted that the lift smelt unusually of aniseed. As the doors closed I said, "Good night then", rather inappropriately as breakfast service was about to begin.

Self-denial, helping others less fortunate than yourself, putting others' needs above your own ... the next fifteen minutes were the nearest I probably ever got to achieving beatification. I fell short of anointing his feet — well who wouldn't? — but I truly felt that just getting him undressed and into bed was way beyond the call of duty. This thorny process was like wrestling with a squid — well, I'm guessing a bit there — and included a rather ill-tempered encounter with one of his new white stretch boots, vaguely and inexplicably fashionable at the time, I recall. One boot in particular didn't seem to want to leave him, for reasons that only a white stretch boot could explain, and I only succeeded by placing my left foot into his groin and heaving with all the strength I had left. Vince's anaesthetic was sufficiently virulent for him not to feel my amateur traction, nor worry that he now had one boot several inches longer than the other. I flopped back against the headboard, and only then did I notice, with dismay, that the bedroom was a bloody double, not a twin. Why should I have expected this part of the accommodation booking to have gone any smoother than the rest?

But now wasn't the time to be barging bolshily downstairs to demand another room. I was exhausted, and the hotel was starting to serve breakfast. So now I had to sleep with Vince too. It's the kind of thing guys are a little uncomfortable with, to be honest. I decided to roll him between the top sheet and blanket, as a TV chef might make a remoulade, or like a spider wrapping a fly. It left me with virtually no sheets, but it was warm, and I was ready to sleep. At 7.30 am, I began to slip into a deep, wonderful slumber — only to be startled back awake within minutes by a hideous, unearthly choking sound from somewhere within Vince's cocoon. In panic I unravelled him, just in case he was actually dying. It didn't sound the worst possible outcome at that time, but I was pricked by conscience. Imagine having to explain to the lads that I heard it and did nothing whilst he lay there choking to death. Bad form. But after a few seconds the choking stopped and he just lay there in saintly repose, calm and untroubled. This, I later found out, was just the way he snores, but it was unlike any snoring I've ever come across, before or since. It was as if he had just one last irritation left in him before I could finally escape into blissful sleep.

All too few hours later, I awoke to brilliant sunshine streaming into the room. I looked at my watch: just gone 10am. Just over 2 hours' sleep. Outside, I could hear scouse accents wafting up to our second floor room from the streets below, debating whether the Hotel Pacific was worth a try, obviously not realising that this was the exclusive preserve of prize winners. From here on, every ferry from England would bring more scousers, a high percentage of them looking for rooms in Ostend. Clearly some had already penetrated the hotel's defences, judging by the familiar accents rising from the breakfast room. I peered out into the achingly bright light. Ostend had become its customary brash, boisterous self after the unaccustomed calm of the early hours. Several hours' more kip would not have gone amiss, but owing to Sleeping Beauty's incompetence in booking a holiday he'd already won, we would need to find rooms for tomorrow evening after the match. Competition would be hot, and delay could be costly. The reason for this less-than-ideal state of affairs snored on, face down, sweating, grunting and oozing stale Pernod. If it sounds bad, you should have been there. Any room-seeking sortie would have to be a solo mission. I was losing count of the reasons to hate Vince, unaware that there would soon be another couple. I decided to have a shower, take a reinvigorating stroll along the sea front and try to find some rooms.

But as I emerged from the shower, towelling vigorously, I noticed that Sleeping Beauty had, by some miracle of metamorphosis, transformed himself into Jack and the Beanstalk. He had turned over onto his back and now lay, seam-up as we cricketers might say, with a gift for womankind — a gift worthy of a better owner, to be honest — protruding proudly through his standard Y-fronts. It was at that precise moment that keys jangled in the door, which burst open to reveal two young and not entirely unattractive chambermaids about their business. Well it was nearly 11 o'clock and they had rooms to clean. And this is the sight that greeted them; one Englishman emerging naked from the shower towelling himself and another lying asleep on the bed sporting The Gift. It took them a second or two to leap to an understandable but horribly wrong conclusion, let out a gasp, clap their hands to their rather exquisite mouths and make a sharp exit, muttering what I took to be apologies in Flemish. Within seconds, the news of the practising English gays caught in the act in Room 5 was being spread amongst all the other presumably attractive young chambermaids gathered on the landing, temporarily silencing the massed ranks of vacuum cleaners. Instead there was just a hushed yet animated, conspiratorial clucking.

It's a sort of male sexual fantasy stereotype, the continental chambermaid in her frilly uniform. Nothing ever happens, but you can dream. Well now as a result of our first fleeting meeting, that dream could be laid well and truly to rest. And still Vince slept on, blissfully oblivious to this latest situation he had put me in. Now I had to endure the acute embarrassment of walking past the chambermaids on the landing with their awful knowledge, still clucking excitedly yet trying to keep their voices low. Trying to explain would only make it worse, I knew. The chattering stopped the second I opened the door. I muttered 'Hello' as I hurried past, eyes fixed to the floor. They managed to suppress laughter for a while, but not quite long enough for me to be out of earshot. Even so, I was anxious not to be out of the hotel for too long in case Vince awoke, saw he was alone, panicked, thought he was still in England (as he had been when last conscious) and caught the next ferry back to Dover. Actually, on second thoughts, the idea could have quickly grown on me ....

The hotel was only a matter of a hundred or so yards from the seafront, and the wind coming off the sea began to sandblast away the cobwebs, travel-lag and hangover. I watched a couple of pure white ferries shimmer towards port on an impossibly blue sea, doubtless carrying a cargo of more Liverpool room-seekers. This steady trickle would become a torrent by this time tomorrow — match day — when the main body of supporters would arrive. Add to those rooms already taken the significant number that would not be open to English football supporters under any circumstances, and our options were already seriously diminished. It was hard not to feel sorry for any ordinary holidaymakers and families, British or otherwise, who had chosen that popular stretch of Belgian coastline for a Bank Holiday break, not realising that they were to be engulfed by hordes of football supporters. Restaurants, bars and cafés, accommodation, transport; all either full or closed, with the authorities on red alert. Wrong place, wrong time.

Yet gazing out to sea in the bright sunshine, I felt an irrepressible surge of optimism, exhilaration and sheer euphoria. Here and now, nothing was really a problem, nothing was insurmountable, nothing and nowhere could be better than this. Although my existence at that moment was not entirely trouble-free, and my problem still lay comatose in bed, no doubt primed to sabotage my every arrangement the moment it regained consciousness. When I returned for an update, having enquired at a few places but failed to find another room — everywhere was full — The Gift had mercifully subsided, although its owner still

snored on in alcoholic oblivion. I went to the hotel bar —
an unaccustomed luxury compared to the basic room-only
establishments we normally stayed in — and ordered a *croque
monsieur,* that peculiar name they give to a cheese toastie,
and a *gueuze,* the name they give to a peculiar but refreshing
Belgian beer that initially comes as a bit of a shock but which
I quite like. Perched on a bar stool with a beer and my toastie
whilst glancing at the English newspapers, I felt more like an
extra from a Noel Coward film than a stereotypical English
football fan. A cigarette smoked rather camply through a
holder would have completed the image.

A guttural scouse accent behind me shattered the illusion.
"Alright dair mate," it said to the barman, "gorrenny aspirins,
me 'ead's fuckin' killin' me."

As the barman began rooting through the shelves in
search of medication, I noticed amongst the clutter the
accommodation register. I decided I'd try to convince them
that they'd made a clerical error, that we should be booked in
for tomorrow night too. I even considered altering the book,
but he might spot that it wasn't his own handwriting.

"You've got us down for tomorrow night haven't you mate?
The name's Bennett. Room 5, tonight and tomorrow, yes?"
Well originally it should have been three, so my request had
honest roots. After all, I was only trying to get one fewer night
than we had originally won for nothing. He studied the book
closely, then a furrow appeared. He looked quizzically at me.
"It is not there," he pronounced solemnly, "I will find out."

"Must have missed it off!" I laughed unconvincingly, as he
disappeared into the staff quarters.

Even a scouser with a hangover knows when you're trying
something on. One wandered over to me and said, "You've got
no chance lad, it's chokka already. I've got four kippin' on me
floor already they don't know about." The barman returned.

He too, it seemed, knew when something was being tried on. "You can stay here tonight, but tomorrow is full. Your room will be occupied. Sorry." But not by us, apparently.

I finished my beer and sandwich and returned to our room to check that nothing stirred — it didn't. I felt frustrated about this inertia, but couldn't just abandon him. Eight of us on this trip and here I was, all on my own. Thinking about it, John's roommate Alan was probably having a similar problem. I went back outside to resume the quest for accommodation. 'All because of Vince's cock-up with his travel agent', was the thought I tried — but failed — to banish. I tried several dives of varying degrees of pokiness, but always the same result: "Tomorrow night? Sorry, we are full." I guess my being English didn't help. I wasn't wearing club colours, but it didn't take a genius to work it out. You rely on finding the places where greed overcomes caution, where someone will take a chance — and your money — presumably in the hope that the gamble doesn't backfire, his property remains unwrecked and possessions remain unstolen. Having again failed to unearth such a local treasure, I took another return to the hotel. This time, oh joy!, it lived, and was crawling out of bed towards the toilet. I decided to defer giving him an update on recent events until I had discovered how much he remembered.

"We're in the Hotel Pacific in Ostend, OK? What do you last remember?"

"The ferry. Pernod. Me and John. I feel shit. I'm goin' for a shower."

"Oh the shower, yeah, that reminds me. The staff here think we're a couple of gays on holiday."

I explained why he might get some strange looks from the chambermaids, but he just thought I was winding him up. I filled in the missing parts of his life story, the bit between now and just after he bought the Pernod. He said we should go and look for rooms for Wednesday night. I explained, calmly, that I already fucking-well had done, several times, without success. We would then, we agreed, get something to eat and get back to the hotel for a few hours' much-needed afternoon nap before our rendezvous with the others at 5pm. We wanted to be in the best shape possible (poor, but still the best possible) for what we knew would be the heavy duty, night-before-the-match boozeathon that this evening would inevitably bring. That was another plan that didn't quite work out.

CHAPTER 5
OUR BIG NIGHT OUT

Tuesday May 28th 1985

If you're not a football fan, it won't surprise you to hear that *haute cuisine* and fine dining play little part in the average football match experience, prawn sandwiches at Old Trafford and Delia's catering at Carrow Road notwithstanding. More often than not, the business of eating is usually reduced to junk refuelling on foot, somewhere in the murky burgers and chips corner of the gastronomic galaxy. Even the act of sitting down to eat would be worthy of comment. Abroad, when faced with unfamiliar menus and languages, and you know, all that foreign muck, this tendency is even greater — well, better the muck you know ....

So for Vince and I to find ourselves seated in a cosy Italian restaurant in Ostend's backstreets that Tuesday lunchtime represented a substantial departure from the Lowest Common Denominator convention. We're used to so much lower than that. We ordered the house speciality, Steaks Florentine-style, and took a guess on some sauces and side dishes. I knew the Italian for mushrooms — though most people could have a stab at 'funghi'. Vince was quickly driven to compete, asking expansively for 'acqua' with an accompanying drinking motion hand gesture, just in case they didn't understand their own language as well as he spoke it. I even ordered wine with my meal, another departure from the customary unrelenting diet of beer. This relaxing, civilising oasis, the good food and drink and comfortable surroundings, with time on our hands and nowhere in particular to be, helped restore a sense of well-being, regulating the body clock and giving the day some shape. The sense of disorientation began to slip away. It's amazing what a civilised meal can do for the human spirit. A couple of hours' afternoon nap, to catch up on last night's lack of sleep and erase the post-prandial sloth, would complete the recovery, ready for this evening's excesses.

But as we made our way back towards our hotel, quite by chance we ran into Phil and Mark, idling along an obscure alley that was nothing but a cut-through to one of the main streets. What are the chances of that happening in a place this size, you wonder? 'Fancy a beer?' 'Well actually we'd rather go back to our hotel for an afternoon nap'. Is the answer you just cannot give. The sarcasm would be merciless. Sometimes it's hard being a bloke. So we said yes, of course, naturally, nothing could be more natural.

Phil then spotted a gruesome-looking Fried Chicken Crematorium across the street, and he and Mark inexplicably fell for its charms. We declined, explaining smugly about having already eaten, about Italian restaurants and steak and wine, and left them to it. There was a bar next to the takeway, and Vince and I were soon positioned by the open sash window, warm sunshine streaming in, cool beer at the ready. Not an unfamiliar experience, nor an entirely unpleasant one, even though a siesta would not have gone amiss.

Now anyone who knows Ostend knows that, whilst no metropolis, it is a substantial sized town, full of sidestreets and backstreets, and — in common with most of Belgium's towns and cities — very well populated. Alan Coren once observed that the Belgians invented the Brussels sprout because it was the only cabbage they could carry home through the teeming streets. So if the chances of bumping into Phil and Mark had been slim, how astronomical must have been the odds of glancing out from that same bar onto that particular tiny corner of Ostend, only to see John and Alan loitering aimlessly past, in touching distance through the open window? You could actually arrange to meet these people and have far less chance of seeing them, as has been amply demonstrated many times before. Vince sprang to his feet and yelled at them through the open window; neither is known for requiring a second invitation to join anyone for a beer.

"Seen any of the others?" asked Alan. We just pointed past the ranks of slowly rotating chickens at Phil and Mark. It seemed John and Alan had had little difficulty finding cheap, reasonable, centrally situated accommodation. They bought a round of beers and sat down beside us, John and Vince chatting conspiratorially about the highs and lows of Pernod addiction. Both looked disappointingly healthy, considering.

Chicken despatched, Phil and Mark sauntered in, spotted the spectre of John and Alan and asked, incredulously and rhetorically, "What the fuck are you doing here?" As protocol decreed, another round of beer was ordered. As any self-respecting British pub goer knows, if you drink in rounds then you stand your round. Therefore, if you're in a round of six like us, the total number of drinks each individual must consume must be either six or divisible by six. Once you've had six, you face the decision of either backing out, splitting into smaller groups or accepting that you now must continue to twelve. Numbers seven to eleven are off the menu. If you don't want to be part of it, or can't afford to be, or plan to leave before the conclusion, or whatever your alibi, you should declare so openly and at the outset, and will probably need an accompanying explanation. This protocol produces surprisingly few problems, provided each individual is aware of it and plays the game, and to a group as synchronised and bristling with common purpose as ours, it was no problem. But it can get muddy when, as now, it just sort of develops and evolves around you, as more and more people join in, and it gets difficult to work out. So although we were only ordering a third beer, and the measures were only half-pints, Vince and I already knew that any thoughts of an afternoon nap were already dead in the hop-flavoured water. Vince and I had not yet bought rounds, and it would be a totally unacceptable breach of protocol to suddenly announce our departure just as our turns became due. Phil and Mark had told us that they too had managed to find a room easily enough, quite clean with a shower, about five minutes' walk from our hotel, only £4 a night (cheap even in 1985). It made our 'free' prize seem even more trouble than it had been worth, and it had been worth quite a lot. For the first time but definitely not the last, I recounted the chambermaids story to the smirking audience.

As we grew more raucous, two middle-aged women sitting nearby became drawn into our ever-expanding and ever noisier circle of chat. Apparently they worked in a local factory and were, they told us with what seemed like indecent haste, married. We bought drinks, exchanged cigarettes, talked about Belgium, about beer, about the football match. Someone in our ranks offered them accommodation for the night, an offer which was politely but quite firmly refused. They already had accommodation, in their own homes with their own husbands in them, thank you very much. When they came to leave, they wished us luck for the match, rose and departed. Vince shouted at them through the window.

"Any jobs going at your place, with your two hour lunch breaks?"

"It's our day off," wafted in the reply.

"Er ... what time did we arrange to meet at the station?" asked somebody or other.

"Five."

"What time is it now?"

"Gone five."

"Whoops. His Lordship will not be amused."

Six glasses were drained, and we hurried to the station to find His Lordship Don and Trisha perched on a wall, legs dangling idly. Everything about Don's demeanour, posture and body language screamed 'not amused'. Don likes to be the organiser of our social lives. He likes to know in advance where we are going and for how long, to tell us when would be a good time to move on to the next place, where we should be finishing up and how we should get there. At home this manifests itself in attempting to organise, or control, transport to matches, the route, the pubs, what we'll have for breakfast and so on. Being excluded, the real reason for his pique, is definitely not on his agenda.

"So let me guess, you've been on the piss since lunchtime? What the frig are you gonna be like by tonight, you amateurs? Ah well, big night ahead boys, let's get on with it. Any plans? Seen anywhere promising on your travels?" He rubbed his hands together in gleeful anticipation of the evening ahead, and the even more lipsmacking prospect of organising it for us.

"Tell you what, let's have a swift dustbuster in this bar on the corner, then shoot up that road, it leads you back into town, there's another little bar just up there on the left ...". He was off, striding purposefully away. Apparently they too had found a room near the station, leaving Vince and I, the accommodation prize winners, as the only ones with no accommodation after the match. Don asked about the Hotel Pacific and Vince's arrival in it this morning. For some reason, it was Vince who asked me to tell them the chambermaid story, as though proud of his part in it. A small part, I should add ....

Cruise liners, apparently, fill from the top downwards, with the expensive cabins always the first to go. Football accommodation is the opposite. The cheaper the hovel, the greater the demand. As most fans are unlikely to return in the same condition as that in which they left, anything beyond a roof, a bed, a toilet and a sink are largely superfluous and hardly worth shelling out for. There are more pressing demands on limited funds, and you are unlikely to be conscious enough to appreciate the finer points of high quality bed linen and a trouser press. In fact, even the bed is arguably optional, as many arrange to just crash out on mates' floors and share the cost of the room. With many thousands of Liverpool room-seekers sure to arrive tomorrow, Vince and I really did face strong competition, but the pre-match night out does not really allow for the luxury of checking out accommodation. Phil suggested there may be a chance of us getting in where he and Mark were staying, but the momentum of the evening soon took over. We would keep our eyes open during the evening, but otherwise try again in the morning.

The night before a big game abroad is the social event of the trip, in purely socialising terms bigger than match day itself. It's all to do with anticipation. You could do the same after the match, especially if your team has won, but by then the plot is revealed, the outcome known, you're on the downward slope back towards normal life. But the night before, it's all still to come, all ahead of you. We reminisced fondly about the pre-match night in Rome a year ago, a tumultuous, unforgettable night of drinking, singing and table-thumping in the city centre and the square around the Trevi Fountain. This time the match wasn't being played in the town we were staying in, so there was a certain sense of detachment from the event, and, well, Ostend is no Rome. But it was lively enough, the air was warm, the sun shone, the beer was certainly better, and we were in a capsule of freedom and anticipation that sealed off the rest of our existence. Ahead lay a long evening of sheer hedonism.

By six o'clock we were having our first beer of the evening — or seventh of the afternoon, depending on how you look at it — in another typical plain, unassuming Belgian café. In Belgium what you drink is more important than where you drink it, an eminently sensible view to me. We chatted about the game tomorrow, the players, the tactics. The tattered remnants of a British newspaper showed that as usual the press were more concerned with the fans than the match, with all the usual alarmist headlines about 'unprecedented security' (unprecedented since the time before, unprecedented since every time an English team plays abroad), rigorous checks for genuine tickets outside the ground, anyone suspected of being drunk refused admittance, massive police operation inside and outside the ground, all bars closed in the city centre and around the ground, and so on, ad infinitum, ad nauseam. We'd heard it all before. The conversation quickly moved on to the dismal Euro-drivel emanating from the whining, wheezing old juke-box in the corner. One record in particular seemed inexplicably popular with the locals, being played over and over. It was called, somewhat perplexingly, Live is Life, and even more perplexingly it entered the UK charts soon after, which I would say is more a comment on the record-buying public than the song.

It comes in stocky little bottles of about two thirds of a pint, with the most unostentatious of labels — no horns or tridents, no licking flames, no warning at all, no hint of the mellow menace that lurks within. Just the word 'Duvel' in red against a white background. Its appearance compounds its capacity to mislead, because although it has an ABV approaching that of a potent barley wine, it has the pale appearance of a *pils ordinaire*, and tastes more like a strong-ish, full-bodied pale ale. It's distinctive, it's delicious and it has the kick of the proverbial mule, though not immediately. It's my belief that they named the devil after the beer, not the other way around. Famed beer writer Michael Jackson described it as "pale as innocence and sinfully deceptive." I had learnt about Duvel the hard way years earlier on a Belgian beer-drinking holiday, and knew to treat it with respect. It's a session beer only for those with an aspirin fetish. Bar staff become edgy when you order it, they frown, tell you to be careful and begin to mumble cautionary tales about its strength, as if they would like you to appreciate this national treasure of theirs without being entirely convinced you are to be trusted with it. Country landowners probably feel the same when forced to open up their crumbling country piles to the day-tripping, crisp-munching, priceless antique-prodding, culturally barren masses.

Perhaps that is why this bar, in common with many in Belgium, did not exactly broadcast Duvel's presence, leaving it to lie in wait on a shelf behind the counter, to be ordered only by the knowing. But I noticed it. And being soppy with bonhomie, thinking nothing could burst our bubble, I started raving about its magical potency. Now, like the deflowering of a maiden or choosing the hottest curry on the menu, drinking the strongest beer available is a challenge that no testosterone-fuelled British males are going to turn down. Inevitably, everybody wanted to try some, a development that would have a profound bearing on the evening, and begin the descent into oblivion of two of our number — although this time not the Pernod twins.

On the whole, the beer was greeted with the same enthusiasm as a Hamas member at a meeting of the Knesset, and most swiftly reverted to Euro-fizz. But two — Phil and Mark — quite liked it. Fired by its fearsome reputation, they ordered another. Then another. That look began to appear in the barman's eyes.

'Be careful sir, it is very strong. Perhaps you are not used to it?' This of course is absolutely the right way to ensure that we stuck with it.

Personally I feel Duvel is a very easy word to pronounce, but even Mark's earliest attempts were as a man who had already drunk half a dozen bottles of it. 'Dooble', 'Dougal' and even 'Bugle' would all make fleeting appearances before the night was out. As if sensing this assault on his previously uncontested title of 'Biggest Threat to the Smooth Running of the Entire Operation', Vince sprang back into life.

"Let's have a bevvy at our hotel bar," he suggested suddenly.

"Er — why?" was the gist of our response.

Because, apparently, he felt an overpowering need to get changed. Everybody else either already had or wasn't going to. But Vince was adamant. He wanted to get changed. So back to the Hotel Pacific we trudged, settling into the unaccustomed comfort of the bar, all dralon and piped muzak, whilst Vince repaired to our room to reattire himself. His reappearance a pint later was spectacular. Out had gone the jeans, T-shirt and trainers, to be replaced by white trousers, white shoes and an attention-seeking Hawaii 5-O short-sleeved shirt. The abuse was as merited as it was merciless. Even the night porter, back for another stint of duty, was moved to comment.

"Ah, you look much better than this morning Mr Bennett."

We headed back into town, narrowly avoiding being mowed down on the pavement by some Liverpool supporters in hired go-karts, yelling "Book 'im Danno" at Vince as they swerved around him. Many other groups of Liverpool supporters were scouring the town's bars just as we were. Passing the doorway to one, an unexpected sound came floating up the stairwell from a dingy subterranean interior. You half-expect the predictable rhythmic thud of dance music that seems to permeate every strand of life, from the local shopping centre to the wound-down windows of the cars doubling as mobile discos driven around by the local lads-about-any-town, kindly sharing the monotonous replica of the industrial workplace with the rest of us. But this was different. Firstly, this was clearly live music, but again not the sort you might expect. No punk or metal merchants, no blues, 60s or Hendrix covers. Instead it was the unmistakeable sound of working men's clubland, more associated with a seedy pub or club in some bleak rainswept industrial side street on a dismal Tuesday evening in the ragged backsides of a northern English town in January, performed by a duo with an engaging name such as Ron 'n' Rick, scratching a living playing to a handful of crusty locals who'd rather be playing darts. It's just not what you expect on a sunny evening on the continent. The sound was of a slightly off-key pub singer vocalist and a cheap electric organ, bristling with Bontempi-ness, both distorted by a PA system that must have come free with petrol tokens. Well you can't turn down a prospect like that can you? Time for some sport.

Down the stairs, we opened the door and peeped inside. In a spacious underground bar with subdued lighting, a sparse gathering, mostly Liverpool supporters, had squashed themselves into a confined space in one corner, watching, or rather baiting, the live entertainment, which consisted of a thin, emaciated middle-aged vocalist, strands of hair plastered by sweat across the top of his balding head with a comb-over *a la* Bobby Charlton, belting out Rock Around the Clock in a heavy Belgian accent. Behind him, surrounded by considerably less technology than a Pink Floyd concert, sat an introverted, bespectacled keyboard player, a little younger and with lank, dark, slicked-back hair and an expression of distinct unease as he glanced furtively and suspiciously at the handful of people dotted around the room. There was something of the Sparks keyboard player about him, except no moustache. Every so often he would glance at his manic mentor for moral support and reassurance.

We thought this might be a laugh for a beer or two. As the song came to a messy, sloppy, unrehearsed end, it drew the sort of applause usually associated with the demise of a wholly unsuccessful batsman in a village cricket match. The band, being troopers, were undeterred.

"OK boyce, now ve play a sonk fur dee furtball", before launching confidently into "Here ve go, here ve go, here ve go."

It was an understandable mistake, I suppose. You could follow their thinking. All those English matches televised across Europe have spawned a continent familiar with the songs and chants of English football. That particular one has been heard with monotonous regularity following its initial arrival into the English game, I think courtesy of Scotland's fans in the World Cup (er, thanks lads). It would be sure to win over the supporters, get them on their side.

Many football songs are more or less universal, but others are attached very strongly to particular clubs, belonging as if by copyright, as much part of it as the stadium and the team. It is out of bounds for other supporters to sing one of yours, except to goad and rile, and your pride wouldn't allow you to sing one of theirs. Birmingham City, Norwich City, Coventry City, West Ham, Tottenham, Southampton, Portsmouth, Stoke City and Liverpool themselves all have their own very particular songs. But of all the songs in all the world for that band in an Ostend bar to pick, it had to be one that had just been recorded by Everton, our arch Merseyside rivals (and incredibly, it charted — another major question mark over the Great British singles-buying public).

It lasted just long enough for it to be recognisable for what it was, before being drowned in a storm of boos, whistles, jeers, flying beer mats and invitations to fuck off. The startled duo just stood there with a "What did we do that was so wrong?" look of bewilderment on their faces. What their misjudgement unwittingly achieved, however, was to coagulate the separate groups of supporters into a homogenous unit. Suddenly it became a football crowd on a night out. It effectively declared proceedings open. It was the night before the European Cup Final, time to let rip. The songs began, the familiar sounds rapidly attracting more supporters down the dimly lit stairwell. The room filled very quickly, and within fifteen minutes the band's further efforts had become increasingly futile. Another round; Phil and Mark continuing the Duvel downward slide, grinning boyishly. We would be staying a while.

As the place filled and the beer flowed and the atmosphere grew ever more rowdy and anarchic, the band limited their ambition from encouraging audience participation — they'd already run aground with that one — to encouraging the audience to sing the same song as them rather than one of their own, but they were engulfed by a tidal wave of singing and chanting, banging of tables and stamping of feet. They gave up, unplugged and went for a beer at the bar, from behind which suddenly appeared a formidable, thick-set woman, stout and stern, the sort of auntie you dreaded as young child — 'give yer auntie a kiss then!' She banged the counter top furiously, her booming voice sounding exactly as you'd have expected it to:

"OK boys, I let you drink but a liddle softer eh, or the police will come and cloce the bar, unnerstand?"

This turned out to be just the first of several increasingly impassioned pleas she made. A semblance of order might fleetingly follow, but by now the genie was out of the bottle. Momentum had developed, fuelled by booze and ever-swelling numbers. By now several hundred supporters were squeezed in to the bar, standing on tables and lined against the walls like starlings on a window ledge at dusk. The walls were draped with red flags and banners, the air warm, wet and heavy, the floor awash with spilt beer and broken glass, light shades swung precariously from the sweat-glistening ceiling. Into the raucous, playful, essentially good-humoured mood of earlier crept an uneasy tension, the sort of atmosphere in which you are never completely sure whether somebody will overstep the mark.

"I don't like the way this is going," muttered Don, still relatively sober, having missed the afternoon's warm-up and resisted the siren call of the Duvel. None of us wanted to be drawn into any trouble, but neither did we want to miss out until this particular party had run its natural course. Another fraught plea for calm produced the unexpected return of the band. How anyone imagined that could be the solution I have no idea.

"OK, now ve quieten sings down vid some shlow sonksh!" I think they said. The keyboard player still looked decidedly uneasy. A voice from the throng shouted for them to play Arrivedercci Roma, Liverpool's anthem from their two Roman triumphs. Not knowing this, they seemed to find the request a little perplexing, but played it anyway. It briefly brought band and audience together, even though they were singing different sets of lyrics. The band looked pleased with themselves at this sudden outbreak of mass audience participation, but the armistice ended soon after the song did, and pandemonium resumed. The bar owner finally cracked. Banging the bar top furiously, hysterically she screamed, "Are you human beinks or English animals?"

The chorus of "English animals!" was predictable and unanimous. They just don't get the intrinsic perversity of the Brits do they? Recognising a lost cause, she resignedly resumed pouring and muttering about the police, though none came. One or two supporters, recognising the situation was getting out of hand, sought to mediate and defuse the tension. One pushed his way to the bar, told her he loved dominant women, publicly and loudly proposed marriage and invited her to start a new life with him in Huyton, one of Liverpool's less photogenic suburbs. "You'll like it there luv," he continued, "you could run me local, the Eagle and Child, it's just like this." It wasn't. It forced a smile from her, and defused the atmosphere a touch. By now the abandoned keyboard was being swarmed over by a horde of amateur keyboard wizards, jabbing their untutored fingers all over the dials and knobs whilst the owner looked on anxiously and a little forlornly.

Then came a cry from the doorway from Duvel-crazed Mark, who had gone outside for some fresh air. "It's the bizzies!" he yelled. The long-prophesied arrival of the local gendarmerie had finally came to pass. The sight of the first uniform through the door produced hushed silence and acute tension — one wrong move on either side, a misplaced comment or joke, and the tinder could ignite. Although booed at the breaking up of the party, the police handled matters sensitively, and the supporters knew not to push it any further. The bar emptied amicably and in an orderly way, ready for its rehabilitation, leaving the owner to reflect on an evening that saw little damage apart from a few broken glasses, no damage whatsoever to human beings (well externally anyway) and handsome compensation from a bulging till.

Outside the bar, several hundred would-be revellers now found themselves on the streets of Ostend looking for somewhere else to play. No more than a hundred yards away, many, us included, were drawn by the sounds of Beatles songs from another bar, muffled except when the doors opened to release a wall of sound and reveal a scene just as chaotic as the one we'd just left. Inside was heaving, airless, hot and all-enveloping. We could get little nearer than just inside

A pre-match stabbing, the recriminations begin

Italian supporters charge towards Liverpool's down the running track at the Heysel

Hours before the game, the mood turns ugly in the Grand Place in central Brussels

Chaos on the pitch for over an hour after the wall broke

UNION EUROPEENNE
DE FOOTBALL
ASSOCIATION

ROMA 25 MAGGIO
STADIO OLIMPICO

COPPA fina
DEi CAMP

CURVA NC
CANCELLO I

005132

Conservare per il controllo

Rome 1977

Paris 1981

FEDERATION FRANÇAISE
DE FOOTBALL

N° 002316

UNION DES ASSOCIATIONS
EUROPÉENNES DE FOOTBALL

FINALE
DE LA COUPE DES CLUBS
CHAMPIONS EUROPÉENS

Mercredi 27 mai 1981 à 20 h 15
au PARC DES PRINCES

TRIBUNE AUTEUIL

Prix : 23 F
Droit de location : 2 F

Total : 25 F

Taxes comprises

onze onze onze onze onze onze onze

FINALE coppa dei campioni

ROMA/STADIO OLIMPICO 30 MAGGIO 1984/ORE 20,15

CURVA NORD
CANCELLO L

0002391

Rome 1984

FINALE

Coupe Clubs Champions Européens
Europese Beker Landskampioenen

HEIZELSTADION

STADE DU HEYSEL

29/5/85

à 20.15 heures - te 20.15 uur

BLOC

PLACE DEBOUT
STAANPLAATS

XY

Non-couverte Niet-overdekt
Côté WEMMEL   Kant WEMMEL

300 Fr.

VAK

TAXES COMPRISES TAKSEN INBEGREPEN

L'organisateur décline toute responsabilité du chef d'accident, de quelque nature qu'il soit,
qui pourrait se produire au cours ou à l'occasion du match pour lequel ce ticket est délivré.
En acceptant ce ticket, le porteur renonce à tous recours en responsabilité contre l'organisateur. — De inrichter wijst alle verantwoordelijkheid af voor ongevallen van welke aard ze
ook wezen die zich zouden voordoen tijdens of bij de gelegenheid van de match waarvoor
dit ticket is afgeleverd. Het aanvaarden van dit ticket betekent voor de houder dat hij van
alle verhaal tegen de inrichter afziet.

Non valable s. souche
Niet geldig zonder strook
Tickets Voet - Deinze

N° 00984

Brussels 1985: even
the ticket looked
unprofessional

80

the door, acting as self-appointed doormen whilst Phil and Mark were despatched in the general direction of the bar — in retrospect not one of our wiser decisions, given they were the two most Duvel-damaged. The epic scale of their task might have deterred less stupefied fellows, but they had reached the stage where nothing was beyond them. They would, they decided, fetch the drinks on piggy-back. As they finally reached the hallowed bar, a loud crash and a huge roar announced that Mark, the jockey, had inevitably dismounted, right onto the bar top, arms and legs scattering glasses and staff, drink and drinkers in all directions.

We just shook our heads and prepared for a long wait for our drinks. Outside, a rival form of entertainment was developing as more police arrived, this time in significant numbers. In an effort to confine the potential for disturbance within this one small area, they had sealed it off with a human barricade across the width of the street. Then they would make sporadic, half-hearted charges down the street towards the bar whenever its doors opened, presumably to terrify and intimidate. But we discovered that, simply by closing the doors again, they would retreat to reform their barricade. Again and again, it worked. Doors open, police charge — doors close, police retreat. It quickly became a sport, a game of chicken, seeing how long your nerve would hold as they advanced before closing the doors again. And we were playing a vital role as we had control of the doors. Rarely can being surrounded and cut off by a foreign police force have seemed less threatening. The police showed a naivety that was almost endearing, and the drinking and singing continued unaffected by the charade taking place outside, though everyone was by now aware of it. A heavier-handed approach would almost certainly have provoked more serious disturbance, so you could argue that they deserved commendation for their sensitivity rather than scorn for their inactivity. Gradually the party wound down of its own accord and ended peacefully.

Within less than twenty four hours, we'd be encountering that same *laissez faire* policing again, but this time with catastrophic consequences.

We headed unsteadily back towards our various rooms, pausing only for a last beer at another typical, sleepy, late-night, strip-lit European bar, one of which's three customers was none other than the vocalist from the first bar, presumably enjoying this tranquil, unpressured sanctuary. He sat alone in a corner, sipping a beer and blowing cigarette smoke slowly towards the ceiling in an enigmatic, arty, insouciant, Jacques Brel kind of way, perhaps reflecting on his unusual Tuesday evening.

His reverie was shattered, not for the first time that night, by Mark's raucous parrot cackle of a voice: "Alright there mate, do You'll Never Walk Alone will yer?", complete with lopsided rictus grin and thumbs up. Just what you want, I imagined, when you're trying to wind down after the stressful experience he'd had earlier. Nevertheless he showed commendable restraint, patience and politeness, just giving us the definitive continental shrug of the shoulders and smiling resignedly. He was happy to chat. "It was not too bad, eh? A little noisy, a little drunk," ... another shrug ... "it was ...OK." A phlegmatic Flem. We drank a beer with him, wished him well and left. It was 3am, which meant most of us had now been drinking for over twelve hours.

Tomorrow was the serious business, and would herald a complete change of mood. The European Cup Final. As big as it gets. If Tuesday was pure pleasure, Wednesday had a large element of business mixed in. After making flimsy arrangements for meeting the next morning, we went our separate ways, Vince and I still needing to find accommodation for the following night. How much easier would it have all been if we could have stayed at the Hotel Pacific for that night too, I wondered for the umpteenth time.

As we bundled glassy-eyed and shiny-faced back into the hotel reception, I felt a somewhat disorientating sense of déjà vu. Same reception, same early hours sort of time, same night light, and same night porter wearing the same expression of mild concern as he glanced over the same spectacles at the same spectacle he'd witnessed almost twenty four hours earlier. Except this time it was both of us. He glanced up, and sized up. We gave him what were probably silly and definitely sheepish grins and, after a futile attempt to cajole him into opening up the bar (at this point his English was substantially better than ours), staggered upstairs. We were in no state to appreciate his softly but expertly delivered parting shot:

"Travel sick again, boys?"

CHAPTER 6
MATCH DAY

Wednesday May 29th 1985. Match day.

It's sad but true — I have never woken up on the morning of any Cup final involving Liverpool and felt well. On top of the obvious physical afflictions — headache, nausea and acute tiredness, caused by, well, over-indulgence, lack of sleep and very poor lifestyle — there's also a curious sense of detachment and unreality, of feeling almost translucent, one dimension removed, as if you're regarding events from outside of your own skin. There's also a little knot in the stomach, of excitement, anticipation, tension, a little bit of fear that you may be about to lose the European Cup Final. You arrive at match day breakfast struggling to recognise yourself.

The weather was unchanged — another painfully bright sunny morning — but the atmosphere today would be very different. Up to now it had been unbridled hedonism, but match day means business. Now we would have to find a different gear, add some form of discipline to the shambolic. Supporting your club means playing a participatory role in the huge occasion ahead; getting behind your team vocally, but also representing it in the city. And another reason for the knotty stomach is the uncertainty over what you'll encounter off the pitch. After all, you're on unfamiliar terrain, at an unfamiliar stadium, with potential threats from three separate sources; rival fans, the police and the locals. We were keen to avoid any such potential flashpoints.

When you're going to an away game in England, you know which part of town a ground is in and the area around it, you know where to go and where to avoid, which pubs are no-go areas full of the home club's baddies. In Brussels all we knew about the Heysel Stadium was that it was in the outskirts. In the '70s and '80s, rampant paranoia formed a large part of the psychology of the English football fan abroad. So established was the English hooliganism 'brand', that the mere presence of an English team and their fans would usually be enough to coax any indigenous psychopaths within a 50-mile radius out of their armchairs and into snarling hostility. Your suspicion that most of the world will be against you is generally accurate, not without good reason. It's fair to say that Liverpool and its fans had some goodwill towards them too; you were just never quite sure which would dominate, the friendly or the hostile. It was certain that Brussels would be very different to cosy, Liverpool-dominated Ostend, safe familiar territory and 100% ours. In the capital, there would be a large and very adjacent support for Juventus, swelled by their access to most of the 'neutral' tickets floating around the continent and the large ex-pat Italian community in Brussels itself. The word was that they would significantly outnumber our own support.

If as fans we were going to put in a professional, streetwise, wits-about-us performance, the early signs in this regard didn't look promising. Vince explained that the fusty, not especially pleasant appley smell that I blamed on an old apple core in the waste basket was in fact the result of his latest atrocity; half asleep and wholly pissed, he had mistaken the shower cubicle for the toilet — this is the cleaned-up version — and parted company with many Belgian francs' worth of the previous evening's entertainment in one almighty go. "Flushed it down the plughole, but some of the chunks got stuck. Still stinks a bit in there", he explained matter-of-factly. I watched in disbelief as he calmly hosed the shower down, prodding about a bit around the plughole before hopping in for his shower. Enchanting.

Breakfast at the Hotel Pacific was a typically continental affair — a choice of excellent coffee or abysmal tea, bread rolls with cheese, jam or something called 'Chokky Spread', which comes in those little individual sealed portions that are easy to open if you happen to have a nuclear device handy, and which taste only marginally better than its name suggests. For most of the succession of bleary-eyed scousers who actually made breakfast, trudging sluggishly across the room, there was only tea, coffee and grunts. In a few hours' time, these were the men whose purpose and indeed duty was to sing their men to glorious victory. The Duke of Wellington's famous quote sprang to mind ....

By 11am on Wednesday morning, Vince and I were packed and out of the 'free' Hotel Pacific, still needing to find a room for that evening. As if to emphasise the different discipline of match day, everyone turned up on time for this rendezvous. The good news for Vince and me was that Phil and Mark had persuaded the owner of their accommodation to release another room for their friends, presumably on the basis that they hadn't wrecked their own the previous evening, though to be fair they'd scarcely been in it long enough to. We followed them to this modest abode and deposited our holdalls. As we left, the owner wished us luck and said he hoped Liverpool won, which was really a sort of verbal household contents insurance policy.

By now the streets of Ostend were like Red Square in Moscow used to be on May Day; red flags, banners and scarves fluttered from every statue and a thousand hotel windows. It made you feel part of something really big and special; the adrenalin rush of supporting a top — *the* top — football team. With our train for Brussels not due for another hour, we found another unpretentious backstreet bar near Ostend station and sat outside for a swift livener and to soak up some sunshine — or catch some rays, as Don would put it. As we sipped, we discussed what we might expect in Brussels. Phil and Vince had had experience of the supporters in Juventus' home town of Turin, having followed England there in the 1980 European Championships. Their account did nothing to quell any apprehensions we may have been harbouring; "These have got some bad boys you know, their Ultras, gangs and knives and everything, faces hidden by scarves. We'll have to be on our guard with these, I tell you." They described the fighting after the Italy-England match in Turin as the worst and most frightening they had ever witnessed. They had ended up barricading themselves into their hotel room with a wardrobe against the door as the sounds of rioting, shouting, screaming, running footsteps, police sirens and even gunshot rose from the streets below.

"Great, well that's cheered everybody up," I said. 'Let's go and get shot.'

Across the street from the bar, we saw many Liverpool fans converging on the station, most clutching packs of beer. Much closer, slumped across a bench outside our bar, lay the comatose figure of another Liverpool supporter, wearing a crumpled green ski-hat (*de rigeur* at the time) and completely out for the count. We paid no attention until a woman appeared, or rather a ramshackle elderly witch with wild, flyaway, corkscrew hair and a bare midriff which revealed a fat, slug-like centre section overflowing her drawstring trousers and which appeared to move independently of the rest of her. She seemed to recognise the slumped figure and greeted it as if it were family, delicately cradling its head and stroking its hair in the most caring way, all the time soothing and clucking gently like a mother hen. Occasionally she punctuated her Flemish jabbering with broken English, whilst the casualty slept on, oblivious to her ministrations. We were too mystified to even speculate at the possibilities in this situation. After a while she picked up a Belgian newspaper. Suddenly she started jabbing a stubby finger animatedly at an article in it, and looked across at us.

"Gooligans!" she squawked, shaking her head and tut-tutting in an exaggerated fashion. "English gooligans!" Then she returned to her unnatural vigil over the still unresponsive ski-hat.

Gooligans. There may be no such word but we felt there really should be. Just that one changed letter seemed to soften the word and make it sound like a cuddly creature from a children's story. You can't really imagine a bunch of gooligans running riot can you? Still, gooligans we apparently were, although we weren't quite sure why. Perhaps there were some reports of trouble last night?

"Oy, who are you callin' gooligans?" shouted Don, laughing.

There was nothing more to do than drink up and head for a nearby supermarket for beer supplies. Time to go to Brussels.

Maybe it's something to do with the acoustics, the amplification, the echo and reverb, but there's something irresistible to football fans about a railway station concourse. The arrival of a trainload of fans is almost always the prelude to hanging out of the windows, banging on doors and yelling their anthems in a ritualistic display calculated to proclaim in no uncertain terms not only their arrival, but their clear ability to take over the town in short order. It is calculated to send decent, law-abiding, God-fearing folk scampering for shelter from the invading army. Highly unsociable really, but it's what happened in the days when the train bore the majority of fans, before planes and coaches and the private motor car took over. For a European final in a foreign city, the motivation is all the stronger, with national as well as club allegiances to demonstrate. Yet on this loftiest of occasions, as our train slid into Brussels Central at just after 2pm, the several hundred Liverpool supporters who emerged from the train did so quietly and unobtrusively, and quickly dispersed, melting away and into the life outside — very much the Liverpool way. Many did not even trouble the ticket collectors. Again, the appearance and behaviour of Liverpool's fans was not typical of English fans generally. Most were dressed smart-casual — designer tops, jeans and trainers — and only identifiable as football supporters by the occasional club ski-hat or lapel badge, and their accents. The good burghers of Brussels continued on their daily business, sparing us only the odd inquisitive glance, scarcely aware that their city had been infiltrated. If, as the media portrayed it, this was a city paralysed by tension and fear of rampaging English football gooligans, then its inhabitants were making a very good job of concealing it.

We parted company with some lads we knew, who had been staying at Blankenberge along the coast north of Ostend, and emerged from the sepulchral gloom of the station concourse into brilliant sunshine. Our first target was central Brussels, and something to eat. We threaded our way through narrow cobbled pathways, and ended up in the upstairs room of a large café bar. Scurrying bow-tied waiters pivoted and swivelled past tables at breakneck speed, plates and dishes precariously but magically balanced and successfully delivered. A babble of different tongues competed — native French, Flemish, English, a few Italians — our first sighting of our rivals. From outside, sporadic bursts of Liverpool songs wafted in on the warm air. Liverpool's supporters still seemed prevalent, despite the expected numerical advantage of the Italians. The atmosphere in the city centre seemed friendly, relaxed and full of bonhomie. On the previous evening a good-humoured football match between the rival supporters had taken place on a campsite on the outskirts of the city, with both sets of supporters regarding each other's clubs with respect at finally coming face to face with such illustrious adversaries. I have rarely, before or since, encountered a less volatile atmosphere than that in central Brussels just five hours before kick-off. In fact it bordered on being anaesthetised, and made what followed even more out of context and all the more difficult to absorb.

For many English football fans, the match is only at the core of a much wider experience involving much socialising and copious drinking — in fact many a good day out has been spoilt by the match. In contrast, for many of our European counterparts the match itself seems the only thing. It's one of many cultural distinctions between English football fans and our continental counterparts. So it was entirely conceivable that many thousands of Juventus supporters would travel all the way from Italy, avoid the city altogether and go straight to the ground, where they would wander around, take pictures and soak up the atmosphere before entering the ground as soon as the gates opened, probably two hours before kick-off. For all but a handful of our supporters, this continental way would be utterly inconceivable. Perhaps crossing that little stretch of water makes the whole experience seem more exotic for us, more of an adventure. The majority of Liverpool's supporters would certainly want to see a bit more than the inside of their transport and a football stadium. As a special concession to a special occasion, we would probably make our arrival at the ground as much as half an hour before kick-off.

In Rome twelve months earlier, there had been the surreal sensation of approaching the Stadio Olimpico twenty minutes before kick-off surrounded only by Liverpool supporters, the only Italians in sight being the street vendors. All 50,000 of Roma's supporters had already been shoehorned into position on the terraces for hours. So whilst the centre of Brussels was dominated by red, with only the occasional black-and-white striped Italian shirt to remind us we were not alone, the roles on the roads and the area around the ground would be completely reversed, as an endless stream of cars and coaches bedecked in black and white headed for the Heysel.

After summoning the bill using the ubiquitous scribbling motion on the palm with an imaginary pen — it seems to work everywhere in the world — we were back on the streets, into a narrow passageway which opened out into the vast, imposing square that is the Grand Place, with its cobbled central market place flanked on all sides by dramatically imposing facades. Liverpool supporters had taken over here too, waving flags and singing in the square and the bars that surround it. But here, the atmosphere was palpably different. An uneasy, brooding calm lay over the square, its cobbled surface poking through an ugly jagged carpet of broken glass and crushed cans, glinting fiercely in the sun. An acrid smell of smoke hung heavy in the air, like the aftermath of some firework display. Right in the very heart of teeming Brussels, everything seemed to have stopped. The people of Brussels, who so far had comfortably accommodated the huge influx of foreign football fans, now seemed fretful and fearful, scurrying around the edges of the square rather than across the middle, avoiding eye contact. Something had happened here, and we wanted to find out what.

We stopped to ask some Liverpool supporters; apparently a jewellery store had been raided, windows smashed, police had arrived, there had been a stand-off between some Liverpool fans and the police, some bottles and glasses had been thrown, the police had fired tear gas into the square, then departed and not returned. It had happened only a matter of minutes before we arrived. It was the first unsavoury experience of our time in Belgium, the first indication that perhaps harmony would not prevail throughout. It unsettled us, and altered the mood, which somehow never fully recovered. Cordial and relaxed morphed into tense and suspicious. Phil, who sniffs the air like a native American tracker, sensed the mood and trusted to his instincts: "Come on, I don't like the look of this. Let's get off."

We decided to leave the city centre and catch the tram towards the Heysel Stadium, maybe get off a stop or two early and try to find a bar — the ones nearer the ground would all be shut, for sure.

Commuter time in the Eurocrat capital is as chaotic as you'd expect, with each mode of public transport engulfed by the human tide, every bus, train and tram groaning as yet more people were shoe-horned in, lurching forwards only to halt a few moments later to disgorge one lot and replace them with another.

I have two theories relating to the world of transport, two Natural Laws that always apply. The First decrees that in every apparently empty space in a car park there will turn out to be a parked small car. It's always hidden by the larger vehicle between you and it, leading you to think you've found a space when you haven't.

The Second Law is that heating and ventilation are inversely proportional to the prevailing climatic conditions. Which means that during a freeze, windows will be jammed in the open position and the heating will be out of order. This being a sweltering late May afternoon, however, windows were jammed shut and the heating for some reason was on.

As our tram approached and squealed to a halt, a standing multitude, swaying and bobbing, clutched out for something to hold on to, like some sort of mass séance. We pushed our way in, the doors closed and sealed us in to ripen in the heat. The tram jolted forward, delivering a thud to the solar plexus and sending half its standing passengers into freefall. The driver seemed a willing, even enthusiastic participant. His idea of personal hell would be to use a clutch. An interminable wait at some lights whilst half of Brussels crossed in front further concentrated the mind on the overpowering heat and airlessness. Rivulets of sweat trickled like the oil bead on the old Castrol TV commercial down cheeks, backs and limbs, faces pressed into the sweat-sodden hair of the nearest passenger. No air, no space, no breeze, no respite. No known anti-perspirant could cope, I don't care what the adverts say.

More sets of lights, more tram stops (eight off, eleven on). On and on it groaned and clanked. A ludicrously overpopulated Fiat zoomed past our ludicrously overpopulated tram, Juventus supporters hanging out of each window, waving black and white flags excitedly whilst the driver repeatedly pumped the horn in true Italian style. We exchanged gestures. After 45 minutes I had grown to despise the infernal tram and its driver and its smelly dank passengers. Hardly a word was spoken, not just amongst us but everybody, all just concentrating on their own little personal private hells. The need to expel the consumed beer added robustly to the misery. At last we decided we were near enough the stadium, and the brutish vehicle slid into our halt to release us. We poured stickily off the tram.

We took a time to regroup, and have a look around. Still no visible sign of the stadium. A toilet, a wash and a beer — in that order — were urgently required, and a bar would cater for all three — except bars near football grounds on European Cup Final day just didn't open, period. We asked a small group of Liverpool supporters nearby, who told us the ground was still a good twenty minutes' walk away, but a small bar was open just around the corner. The news was as welcome as it was surprising. It would doubtless be packed and a nightmare to get served in — any open bar would be quickly discovered and descended upon by the hordes. But so out of the way was it, it was actually blissfully quiet, an almost monastic refuge of coolness and serenity.

After a rugby maul to use the single toilet, we settled down for one of the most refreshing cold beers of all time, and despatched it almost instantly. We purchased replacements and took them outside into the glorious late afternoon sunshine, where Don the sun zealot immediately rearranged the benches to form a sort of sun lounger. Off came the shirt to reveal bare torso, in finest gooligan tradition. The rest of us just sprawled across the pavement in the heat of the afternoon, backs propped against the wall, idly watching the world go by and contemplating the last few moments of tranquillity before the maelstrom that was ahead. Here we were, not much more than two hours before the European Cup Final, sunbathing and taking photos like we were on summer holiday. There would be no point trying to get a beer any closer to the stadium, all the bars would be closed.

On the main road about two hundred yards away at the bottom of this quiet side street, we could make out the traffic flowing Heysel-wards, mostly car- and coach-loads of Italian supporters, all air-horns, flags and excitability.

Vince broke the unnatural calm: "Where the fuck is everybody?"

"Very poetic" grunted Don, adjusting his pose for an even tan. Then he sat up sharply, pointing down the street, and shrieked: "Look at the fuckin' state of that!", very poetically.

We followed his finger to its very obvious target, a shambling, drunken wreck of a figure trying with spectacular lack of success to walk up the road. In his highly advanced state of alcoholic stupor, he swayed and staggered unsteadily, sometimes forwards, mostly sideways, occasionally crashing into a cunningly disguised solid object such as a wall and bouncing off again. It reminded us of — well, Vince and John a day and a half earlier. This manifestation had long, lank hair that had recently been washed in French dressing, a bare torso and a spot-infested face and neck that resembled a photo of the moon's surface. A union flag dangled from his waistband, over which flopped a huge, fat, wobbly gut. In a final affront to style and decency, he wore baggy, shapeless, massively flared jeans, down one leg of which was written 'Liverpool F.C.' Oh how proud he made we fellow fans feel!

Don, a body fascist, eyed this repulsive specimen of humanity with disgust. "Look at that horrible fat bastard!" he yelled, cruel as child in a playground, though not technically incorrect.

"When did you teach him the walk then, Vince?" laughed John, which was rich coming from him.

That our fellow supporter seemed to be travelling alone did not seem entirely surprising. As he drew closer, we could hear him muttering and singing to himself, an incoherent rambling that we recognised nothing of. The international language of the tramp, perhaps? Sadly, the mutant mistook the laughing and the English voices as kindred spirits and an invitation to join us, and lurched towards us with a painfully deliberate thumbs-up. With a totally inexplicable sense of pride he announced: "I am a German. I am from Munster. Vorwaerts Liverpool."

So this shambling epitome of the English football fan turned out to be German.

"You are a Munster more like", added Phil. 'Piss off will you, mate?'

He complied, with some disappointment but to our great relief, and wandered off in the vague direction of the ground. He'd have been just perfect for stoking stereotypes and reinforcing prejudices back home about what English fans abroad are really like; any British tabloid photographer would have greedily snapped him up. The next day, everyone at home could have shaken their heads, tut-tutted and declared that this was just typical of English football fans, these people are scum, why do we produce them and the foreigners don't? Well here was proof that they do.

The leading handful of English clubs have an appeal and a support that is literally worldwide. Liverpool themselves draw support from a vast, cosmopolitan, multi-racial base encompassing every continent. Later we would see Dutch, French, Bulgarians, many Scandinavians including coach loads of red-shirted Danes with 'Danish Dynamite' across their chests and 'Liverpool FC Supporters — Copenhagen' on the backs of their coaches. There were Maltese, and Africans and Caribbeans and Asians and Mauritians, and those who had travelled from North America and Australasia. And of course from Munster, Germany. Add the Welsh, Scots, both parts of Ireland and all parts of England and you get some idea of the vast polyglot support that was descending on the Heysel Stadium from a thousand different starting points with one common aim — to see Liverpool win the European Cup.

We knew there'd be no point trying to find another bar open so close to the ground, so we bought some cans from a nearby shop and sauntered off in the direction of the stadium. Rounding a sweeping bend, we joined the main approach road to the stadium from the centre of town, the Avenue Houba de Stroupa, and caught a first thrilling glimpse of the stadium, gleaming in the sunshine. Lining both sides of the road were the usual match day paraphernalia — stalls selling flags and team colours, the evocative and pungent aroma of hot dogs and burgers, the shouts of the street vendors, the traffic now backing up, the pavements busy with fans heading on foot towards the ground. Still an hour and a half before kick-off, still very early for us.

Fifty yards ahead of us, a commotion suddenly broke out at a hot dog stall. A small group of Liverpool supporters were shouting angrily and gesticulating at a hot dog vendor. The cause suddenly became sickeningly apparent. A young man in Liverpool colours lay on the grass verge in obvious distress. One leg of his jeans glistened dark and wet from thigh to knee. Sometimes the human brain struggles to rationalise the message the eyes are sending it, and seeks to repel such an ugly, steely intrusion on fluffy existence. But there was no doubt; somebody, right here in front of us, had just been stabbed. Then comes the adrenalin surge; senses switch to hyper-alert, eyes scanning, brain processing; are we in danger too? Wrong place, wrong time? The injured man's friends gathered round and tried to comfort, a crowd quickly grew, those nearest the scene asked questions, and didn't like what they heard. Fingers pointed, voices were raised, accusations, threats and obscenities flew, running footsteps clattered on tarmac. A group of Liverpool supporters sprinted towards the hot dog stall. A fight started, blows rained in, dull, fleshy and sickening. The hot dog stall was rocked and rocked, side to side, until it began to topple over, sending hotdogs, burgers, bread rolls cartwheeling into the traffic-choked road, followed by a spreading slick of scalding water; some drivers swerved to avoid the scene; others slowed down to get a closer look. Startled onlookers were frozen in the moment. The hot dog vendor, backing away from his assailants and visibly terrified, suddenly produced a long knife; somewhere in the distance, sirens began to wail and lights flash — it was to be the soundscape for the rest of the evening. Tyres screeching, the police arrived, followed seconds later by an ambulance. The injured man was carefully stretchered in, the hot dog vendor bundled less carefully into a police van. They sped off, the crowd began to disperse and the traffic to inch forwards again. The story we heard later was that the hot dog vendor had accused someone of stealing from his stall, an argument had developed and got out of control, he'd stabbed the youth in the thigh, and that's when we had arrived.

But the rumour that began to spread like a bush fire amongst Liverpool's supporters was different; that a Liverpool fan had been stabbed by an Italian, or a group of Italians, all carrying knives and looking for trouble. The Chinese Whisper gathered frightening momentum, this apparently unprovoked attack on an innocent Red turning the mood around us very ugly.

Just like in the Grand Place, we had arrived seconds after a disturbance. It was about to happen a third, catastrophic time.

CHAPTER 7
AT THE HEYSEL

May 29th 1985, 6.30pm-after midnight

I've no idea what the Heysel Stadium is like now; it's not even called the Heysel Stadium anymore. But on the day that it made history, it was a rickety, ramshackle, crumbling, run-down football and athletics stadium in the north-western part of the Brussels conurbation. Its history involved some Belgium international matches and domestic cup finals and some athletics meetings. It was rarely more than half-full and usually less than that. This time it would be full to its nominal capacity with nearly 50,000 supporters.

Close behind the Heysel Stadium stands one of Brussels' most distinctive landmarks, the Atomium. Built for the Brussels World Fair in 1958, it's a huge metallic reconstruction of the atom, rising hundreds of feet into the sky and instantly recognisable to anyone who has driven around the Brussels peripheral motorway ring. For me it remains to this day a stomach-churning memorial to that monstrous night. Just seeing its image, even if only in a brochure or newspaper article, is enough to set off a small hand grenade in my stomach and vividly reactivate all those recollections. But on that perfect late spring evening, the Atomium rose majestically into the vivid blue sky, its metal glinting in the sun's glare. In the foreground, the flags of the Heysel Stadium fluttered proudly in proclamation of its finest ever moment, the first time it had ever hosted the major European final — and its last. No scene could have hinted less at the sordid, squalid show that was to follow.

The Heysel was approached by a series of pathways winding through lawns and gardens adjoining the main road. As expected, the entire area was a ring of steel barricades and temporary fencing, each break manned by police with dogs. Here supporters would be checked for alcohol, weapons and valid tickets before being allowed closer to the stadium. Beyond, much nearer the ground, a second inner ring would pick off any who had somehow evaded the first search. At least that was the assumption, and all perfectly customary procedure for football fans.

What certainly wasn't customary on that day was the sight, in full view of hundreds of on-duty police, of several bars open right by the ground and, hardly surprisingly, packed to bursting point. As this was Liverpool's end of the ground, it was a red and white carnival, with supporters spilling out onto the road and massed on the wall. From inside came all the familiar anthems amidst a cacophony of shouting, foot-stamping and table-thumping.

Throughout the late 1970s and 1980s, pubs and bars by a football ground and inside it were closed on match days, without exception, and especially in Europe when an English club or the national team was involved. It was, on police orders, the (reluctantly) accepted norm. You were lucky if the whole city didn't close. So to see these bars open, right in front of the police, was a culture shock for us, albeit a very welcome one, and all but unprecedented for such a big game in Europe, defying all logic, wisdom and common sense, and contradicting every assurance from all the authorities. But if life is made up of fixed and variable factors, that hordes of football fans will take advantage of a bar open right by a stadium is definitely one of the former. Leave the chicken coop open and the fox will certainly get in. Despite the strong advice — rather than enforcement, transparently — not to open, the lure of quick fat profits was presumably enough for the bar owners to take the risk of damage, disturbance and adverse publicity. That's market forces for you I suppose — if somebody wants something and is prepared to pay for it, somebody else will be prepared to supply it, regardless of the consequences. Opening was a decision based on straightforward, calculated self-interest, and, purely from the commercial point of view, a successful one. The profits would more than pay for a few hours of the cleaners' time. But it was astonishing, in the context of the times and given the high profile of the match, that they were allowed to open, by both the police and the Brussels authorities.

We felt like children with our noses pressed against the outside of a sweet shop window who had suddenly been invited inside to tuck in. It was a wholly unexpected opportunity to grab another beer and let rip with some singing and chanting to get in the mood, a last chance to crank up the atmosphere before the match. We weren't going to miss it. We entered the first and biggest bar. Inside the insane, heaving melee, the mass of bodies had almost fused into a single pulsing entity. Within seconds, our shirts were soaked with sweat and beer that spilled from plastic glasses held on high as people tried to push and worm their way through. The toilets had long since ceased to cope, and a trail ran from them to the pavement outside. The super-competitive business of getting served was only for the grimly determined or desperate, but we managed it. The story of the stabbing had arrived before us, fuelling the tension that hung heavy in the overpowering hot stale air. There also seemed to be any number of obviously forged tickets in existence, wads of them being passed around in tens and twenties at a time, with the instruction: "Get something for them if you can, or get your mates in, or just dump them." For once, supply seemed to outstrip demand, as handfuls of discarded forgeries were tossed idly aside, fluttering earthwards to be trampled soggy. Forgeries are always an ominous harbinger of trouble; if they work and get people in, they can cause serious congestion. If they don't, they can cause delays and unrest at the turnstiles or at whatever point the forgery is detected as people are turned away, or try to break through by force, or turn nasty, or get arrested.

With about half an hour left to kick-off, we drank up and left for the ten-minute walk to our end of the stadium. The first security check, the most cursory and superficial of body searches, revealed a disinterest that almost bordered on the insulting to fans from the country that consistently topped the hooligan export league. We did not know yet, but these same security checks at the other end of the ground were failing to detect a replica handgun, which later turned out to be a starting pistol ("Ooh it's not a gun it's a starting pistol, OK fine you can bring it in then, no problem"), to be brandished at the height of the carnage by an Italian supporter before a worldwide TV audience of millions. No other security check followed this one. We just passed right through the sets of barricades, police didn't even stop us or ask for tickets. Suddenly we were on our final approach. Away to our right, we could see part of our crowd in one of the terraces, a vast curving sweep of red and white bathed in sunlight. We followed the signs for Blocks X and Y, past the main stand and up a gentle slope. We didn't quite know what to make of the muffled thud that soon followed, not crisp enough for a firecracker, not metallic enough for clanging gates, not quite like any of the usual football match sounds.

Suddenly, ahead of us, a group of supporters came clambering over the wall at the edge of Block Z, shouting and gesticulating. At first we assumed it was our lot trying to bunk in without tickets and being turned back. More and more appeared, swarming over the wall and charging down the bank towards us. But as they drew nearer, running maniacally towards us, it quickly became apparent they were not Liverpool supporters trying to get in but Juventus supporters getting out. And they were heading straight for us, at speed, maybe a hundred or more. When faced with a number of rival supporters charging at him, the average English football fan's experience tells him they are not coming for his autograph.

Phil's eyes narrowed: "Bloody hell, these are coming for us here — quick, get a brick or something!" The first group arrived, but just ran straight on past us, wild-eyed, before barging into some more Liverpool fans behind us. One Italian, wearing a silk scarf like a headband, bandanna-style, launched into a bizarre kung-fu routine with circling hands and trilling noises, before sprinting off with the others. More and more followed, all with the same wild demeanour. Most odd, we thought, not familiar with this type of pre-match behaviour, as we continued towards our entrance, completely unaware of the significance of what we had just seen and heard.

Our first sight of the crumbly stone walls and old-fashioned turnstiles conjured an image of rosettes and rattles, Kenneth Wolstenholme commentary and the old 'Match of the Day' theme tune. It was tragi-comic to behold, like a faded glamorous actress long past her prime auditioning for the part of sex kitten. Outside the shabby exterior, an anarchic, unsupervised queue swayed and swirled without pattern as it shoved and pushed and sweated towards what seemed a wholly inadequate number of turnstiles. Many of those forged tickets were being used successfully. We witnessed cash being handed over to turnstile operators who then allowed them in. The sacred match ticket, that took so much hard work to get hold of, seemed to have been relegated to an optional extra for this strictly ticket-only event. In another major departure from convention, there were no police or stewards outside to control the surging swaying mass, or just beyond the turnstiles to check and control the access points. As the pressure at the front of the queues built, those behind were crying out for the pushing to stop — a chilling foretaste of what was to come four years later at Hillsborough.

Having finally got into the stadium, further reasons for the turnstile chaos immediately presented themselves. Just beyond the turnstile, a water pipe had fractured, turning the area into a sea of reddy brown mud, in which floated endless crushed paper cups and empty cans, discarded wrappers from chocolate bars and bags of crisps and other unidentifiable debris. A red Liverpool FC cap lay forlornly semi-submerged. The mud lake was too wide to jump across, so wading was the only alternative. The result: apart from spattered jeans and squelchy shoes and socks, it meant a build-up of bodies just beyond the turnstile, restricting the smooth flow of supporters into the ground from outside, at the precise time and place where the crowd pressure was greatest.

Once over the water jump, the next obstacle was a choking, swirling cloud of red dust, as the decrepit building's foundations were scuffed into life by the stampede of thousands of pairs of feet. Ahead of us, partly no doubt as a result of the cavalier approach to ticket control and ground admission, the terracing was a solid, impenetrable Red Sea with no parting — and there were still thousands outside waiting to get in, most presumably possessing genuine match tickets and assuming there would be space for them. But they, like us, would have to lever their way through, prising bodies apart and wedging their own into the tiny gap created, which would snap shut instantly behind them as they pushed forwards another few inches in the sweltering body heat. On some of the crush barriers, the concrete had crumbled away to reveal the exposed metal reinforcing strips inside, rusted and twisted.

We felt an acute sense of disappointment at the standard of the venue; this stadium did not make it feel like European football's grandest occasion. You expect to be impressed, awestruck by the sense of occasion; I thought back to the grandeur and pageant of the Stadio Olimpico in Rome, the inspiring first impressions and the explosion of sound and vision created by Liverpool's army of fans. In stark contrast, the inglorious Heysel felt second-rate, squalid, shorn of style and class, and with feeble organisation to compound it.

We finally found a position where we could see what should have been the green of the pitch. Instead, we saw that the entire near right-hand quarter of the vivid green playing surface had been engulfed by a human spillage of epic scale — a tangled mass of fans, police, stewards, officials, paramedics and photographers. We took this as nothing more than yet another manifestation of overcrowding and organisational incompetence. After all the chaos, Don began to lose patience, with which he probably isn't over-blessed: "For fuck's sake sort yourselves out, this is shite", he yelled across the terraces.

"There's been a bit of bother in that corner lad, a crowd surge or something, a bit of fighting like", came a voice from behind. If the match was to start on time in twenty five minutes — 20.15 kick-off in those days — there was an awful lot of clearing up to do. In the UK, a TV audience of millions was finishing dinner, fetching beer from the fridge and settling down to watch the football. But what they, and millions more across Europe and across the globe, saw and heard instead were the first harrowing images of people dying at a football match. Replay after replay of clashes and charges between rival supporters was being shown, interspersed with an ever-rising fatalities figure. Around the globe, newsrooms sparked into frenzied activity, phones and faxes chattering excitedly as a major news story broke. Yet we inside the Heysel Stadium, only yards from the eye of the hurricane, had much less idea of the gravity of the situation than most of the rest of Europe who were watching. No commentary, no replays, no access to TV or the authorities to feed us information, certainly no rumours of deaths yet, just speculation. Still oblivious to the nature and scale of the incident, we remained the calmest and least horrified of observers. I'm sure it looked incredibly callous, but we just didn't know. We just wanted the pitch cleared so the European Cup Final could start, and grew more agitated with the authorities' apparent inability to get even that right.

Despite the frenzied scurrying and frantic arm-waving of the assembled legions of arm-banded officials, police and the advance guard of the army, the situation seemed not to change for what felt like an eternity. Their hyperactivity contrasted sharply with the unnatural calm that had settled over the red mass of supporters. With kick-off so close, excitement levels should have been approaching critical. Instead we waited in silence for news, explanation or action, or at least some visible signs of progress. Kick-off, if indeed there was going to be one, would clearly be considerably delayed, opening up the additional complication of probably missing our last train back to Ostend.

A man wearing a Liverpool shirt suddenly appeared on the running track surrounding the pitch, hotly pursued by another supporter. After being chased for nearly half the length of the pitch, he was felled by a brick to the head. The pursuing police seized the chasee — though not the chaser — and frogmarched him away with highly visible and almost over-compensatory firmness for their hitherto supine response. Cops chasing fan chasing fan, it was a farce that belonged more to The Benny Hill Show than the European Cup Final.

There would clearly be no football for some time. We decided to move to the back, away from the packed terracing, to find some less competitive oxygen. It also gave us a clearer view of the chaos on the pitch. Two concentric semi-circles of armed police with helmets and riot shields now spanned the entire Liverpool section of the crowd, staring blankly back at us with their backs to the pitch. Whatever had happened, it looked pretty clear where the blame was being apportioned. With all the police attention directed towards us, the Juventus crowd remained a police-free zone. A rhythmic chant rolled out from the Italian masses, thousands of black-and-white flags jigging suddenly into life. One bore the inflammatory message 'Reds are Animals'. Unless someone had brought a blank flag and felt-tip marker pen in to the stadium with them, ready to tailor a relevant message on the spot according to events as they unfolded, at least one Italian fan had a preconception regarding the English fans opposite them.

A few red flags waved half-heartedly in token, muted response, but by now nobody seemed in the mood. A large electronic scoreboard — just about the stadium's only concession to the 20th century — flashed incomprehensible digital messages, whilst a public address system babbled incessantly and totally unintelligibly. A mood of deep gloom and foreboding pressed down like a heavy, soggy blanket. All we'd looked forward to for so long, built ourselves up for, dissipated into the clammy evening air.

By this time, at the opposite end of the ground, a group of Juventus supporters had got to work dismantling the perimeter fence, but the police, preoccupied with staring at us, either didn't notice or didn't care. A group broke through and swarmed over the mangled debris of the fence. Another roar rolled from the Italian end as a group of 40 or 50 began to charge round the running track towards our end. *(See photo page 79.)* We watched with mild bemusement. A crowd of 15,000 does not feel threatened by 40 or 50 potential attackers, but the evening was becoming more surreal by the minute. It was tempting to shout a pantomime-style "Behind you!" to the police, who steadfastly refused to switch their expressionless gaze from us as the Italians grew ever closer behind them. Some of the Italians wore scarves bearing the *Ultras'* skull-and-crossbones insignia, pulled cowboy-style over the mouth and nose.

When they reached the seated Liverpool section they came to a halt and began hurling stones, coins, cans, even a metal waste bin into the packed seating. The response from the Liverpool supporters was immediate, and a random assortment of debris (including the returning waste bin) arced from the stand towards the Italians on the running track, who scattered to ironic jeers as the bin crashed to earth and bounced amongst them like a loose firework.

Most of the police continued to ignore the entertainment from a distance of no more than twenty yards away, but eventually one or two began to take a mild interest, tilting their heads ever so slightly away from us and towards the skirmish behind them on the running track. A detachment finally broke away and another half-hearted cartoon-style chase ensued, to get the errant Italians back down the running track to their allotted territory, accompanied by jeers of derision. The Olympic 4 x 100 Police Chasing Fans event. Lane discipline was poor.

By now, large sections of the perimeter fence at the Juventus end of the ground were under assault. No longer able to ignore the growing disorder, a large contingent of police was despatched towards it from somewhere within the bowels of the stadium. Dressed in curious blue overalls and helmets, they looked more like armed plumbers than crime fighters as they marched purposefully towards the Italians, to more ironic cheers from Liverpool's supporters. They were immediately bombarded with debris — there was now plenty of it lying around — by the Italian fans and, seriously undermanned, they mounted a swift and decisive retreat.

The apparent timidity of the Dyno-Rod police seemed to further encourage the Italian fans, who this time mounted a major pitch incursion; with many hundreds now on the pitch behind the goal and around the penalty area. More reinforcements arrived, with what seemed like divisions of militia marching formally and grandly into the stadium, only to be stricken by the same lethargy and indecision that afflicted their colleagues. The battle waged on as the rest of us watched on, totally bemused yet bizarrely entertained by this degeneration through anarchy towards farce. There was still no sign of the football, and we still didn't know what had happened or why there was this interminable delay in getting the game started. It was clear something major had gone wrong, but we still had no idea what.

The pitch at our end was by now all but clear, with all

the disturbances at the opposite end. By now the story had begun to circulate that some fans may have died after a wall collapsed following some charging across the terraces. Somebody behind said an appeal had been broadcast for the Italian fans to identify the bodies, but nobody knew whether that was true; rumours have a way of developing a life of their own as we'd already seen earlier that evening. But if it was true, you could only imagine the affect such an announcement would have had on our own fans if the roles had been reversed. Increasingly it became obvious that we were in the presence of something momentous, something extraordinary, that would be enough to dwarf the almost continuous civil disobedience we had been witnessing — normally more than enough to be the main event of note — as well as severely delaying or maybe even causing the cancellation of Europe's most prestigious footballing event.

I went to the toilets at the back of our terracing, where a distressed Merseyside coach driver was talking to another fan. Apparently he had been back to his coach and picked up BBC commentary on the coach radio. "They're saying there was some fighting in the corner there, and a wall's collapsed and loads got trapped. They reckon there could be more than 20 dead ...". He looked the solid, dependable sort, not prone to flights of fancy. I stared, uncomprehending, disbelieving, at the scale of what I'd heard, and walked away in a daze. The news circulated rapidly around the Liverpool terraces. Flags and banners were lowered, and the fans became still and silent, with scarcely a sound emanating from 15,000 people, who just stared out glassy-eyed towards the pitch, trying to grasp a hideous truth that was just too big to deal with.

As regular football-goers we had become accustomed over the years to some large scale punch-ups, some missile-throwing, and occasional stories of someone you know getting hurt. But there was no precedent for deaths — mass deaths. The Heysel Stadium, now brilliantly illuminated like a spaceship against the encircling black night, had suddenly become the centre of the world's media attention. Outside in the darkness, helicopters buzzed angrily, their lights twinkling in the night sky, and sirens wailed. The thought that they could be ambulances heading for the city morgue chilled to the bone. The PA system continued to babble indecipherably. Apparently the two team captains broadcast an appeal for calm, but nobody I have ever spoken to — during or since — even heard Phil Neal's voice.

Through the unnatural calm you could hear snatches of conversation:

"They can't play the match now, it would be wrong."

"It wouldn't finish until after midnight anyway."

"They've got to play it tonight, there'll be murder outside if they don't".

"There'll be murder anyway."

"I couldn't give a shite about the match, I just wanna get home."

"They'll let everything calm down, call the match off and escort everyone away."

"I just wish they'd tell us what's going on."

"They'll throw the book at us for this. We'll cop the blame for every hooligan for the last twenty years for this."

Certainly the imminent prospect of sharing the streets and buses and trams with over twenty thousand enraged, revenge-seeking Italians did nothing to lift the mood. A long and uncertain night lay ahead. We felt a long way from home, and safety. However, of two things we could be certain: in the short term, we were going to miss the last train from Brussels back to our rooms in Ostend; and long-term, this would be the last time we'd be watching Liverpool in a match in Europe for a long time.

Suddenly, completely unannounced — or if there was an announcement, nobody heard it — the two teams walked onto the pitch, side by side, without ceremony and nearly two hours late. The applause that swept around the stadium was of relief rather than excitement; relief that something was at last happening, relief that for ninety minutes at least there would be something else to think about. Flags danced demonically if half-heartedly to life again. The agonising wait and uncertainty were, temporarily at least, over. At nearly ten o'clock at night, there would after all be a football match. Apparently it had been decided to conceal the full seriousness of the evening's events from the Liverpool players in order to persuade them to come out and play at all.

For the record, as if it matters, it was a poor game — what else could it ever have been? For players and supporters it could never be a proper match. We still didn't have much in the way of detail, but everyone now accepted that many lives had been lost just a matter of yards away to our right. One of the beauties of football is that you forget about everything else for ninety minutes, but not that night. Nobody around us really cared much about the game, and hardly watched it. Lost in thoughts, you'd look up and see another three minutes had been played. Some Liverpool fans left early, even as early as half-time, a few even earlier, and handfuls continued leaving throughout the match, no longer interested in the outcome. I don't think they missed much. Juventus won 1-0 with a distinctly dubious penalty, but the match was now merely the precursor to what to us had become the main event: how to get safely back to Ostend.

Opinion is still divided about whether they should have played the match. If you think that a match could not possibly matter after such a horror, of course you're right; it couldn't, and it didn't. But I believe that if the authorities got one decision right, it was this one. For a start, playing the match bought some time; about two hours' worth, to be precise. Time to get more police and army into position, in the town centre and the main transport hubs, as well as in and around the ground. Time to think about how to handle what had already happened, and time to work out how to avoid the imminent conflagration of putting 50,000 rival fans onto the streets simultaneously, and how to get them out of Brussels and out of Belgium. Most of all, time for some of the thunderhead of tension to dissipate. I honestly believe that to have announced, after all that delay and uncertainty, that there would after all be no game and we could all go home, would have courted further disaster. It may have seemed disrespectful, even sacrilegious, to play, but the alternative could have been much worse. Why was the game played? It was public morality v public order, and in this decision to play the game, public order won.

The evening had left us all utterly drained, emotionally castrated, and all the while, as the match wore on, there was the sickening fear, nibbling away at whatever we had left, of what may still lie ahead. The moment of truth was getting closer by the minute. With about five minutes of the match remaining we decided to make our move. What if Liverpool equalised, then went on to win in extra time? Well so what? We filed quietly, furtively, out of the wretched Heysel and off into the dangerous Brussels night, senses super-primed. All the rules of civilisation, all the myriad social conventions that keep our species from anarchy, the fragile veneer that separates us from the savage, were temporarily in suspension. We felt the primal fear of being alone, feral, utterly self-reliant, having to fend for ourselves in an environment supercharged with hostility and vengefulness. If we ran into trouble, we had only ourselves to get us out of it. The law of the jungle, survival of the fittest, relying on primal instincts … no good expecting the police to come to our aid after what we had seen of them. As it turned out, they weren't there anyway, virtually the entire uniformed contingent of Belgium presumably still being inside the stadium.

A hundred yards or so down the road, we heard the muffled roar that signalled what must have been the final whistle and the Italians' victory. It also suggested that most of the Juventus supporters were still inside the ground, just where we wanted them to be. The presentations and ceremony would just give us a few more minutes' advantage. But we still had to contend with the centre of Brussels, where many of the crowd would inevitably congregate. Well, after all, if you were an Italian fan intent on revenge, that's where you'd head for, knowing that most of ours would have to be there.

Inside the stadium, the huge, glittering European Cup, that incomparably majestic trophy, was being presented to the Italians, their delirious fans strangely ecstatic in the circumstances, their end of the ground a seething, boiling mass of flags and flares burning bright scarlet; partly, perhaps, because it was the first time they had ever won this proud trophy, but partly no doubt because they had triumphed over the red evil.

We walked quickly and apprehensively through the raw, unprotected streets, where instead of the usual post-match hubbub, a silent curfew prevailed. Half-walking, half-jogging, moving quickly and as unobtrusively as we could, we tried to keep a few minutes ahead of the bulk of the crowd. No bus, tram or taxi was around to offer any respite from the intimidating darkness, where every set of footsteps, every shadowy group of figures held menace. An anxious glance behind, ahead, left and right, constantly sniffing the air for danger, checking, checking, always checking, senses working overtime, being carried forward on auto-pilot, battling to keep our imaginations in check and the nightmarish possibilities at bay. We were well and truly spooked by this point. As we were far too late for the last train back to Ostend, we had decided to set about the long haul back to the centre of town, for the sanctuary of light, of people. We would make for the main railway station and spend what was left of this wretched night there before catching the first train out in the morning. We even discussed keeping a duty watch, except of course that sleep would be out of the question anyway. However, events took a different course.

Suddenly, running footsteps behind; we spun round, blood pumping, knuckles tightened. The first figure was almost upon us. "The specials are this way boys," gasped a scouse voice. We didn't have tickets for the football special trains, only for the normal service trains, but our desire to get out of Brussels superseded any such technicalities. The special trains would inevitably go to Ostend for the ferries back, so we would argue about it later if we had to. Besides, surely the Belgian authorities' desire to get us out of their country as quickly as possible would override any petty concerns about valid train tickets?

Driven by pure adrenalin, we followed the gang of running youths to a railway station called Jette, a district of Brussels adjacent to Heysel. A long train was waiting at the platform. Sweating and panting, we dived on, crammed ourselves into a compartment, drew the blinds to door and window and collapsed, mentally and physically drained. Still nobody spoke, all stunned, trying to come to terms with what had happened during the last few hours. I glanced at my watch. After midnight. At last our immediate physical environment seemed secure, and the relief was indescribable. Don lifted the window blind to reveal hordes of Liverpool supporters now descending upon the station and packing into the train, a sombre, dispirited, beaten army, bewilderment and exhaustion etched onto pale, drawn faces. It seemed the train could take no more, but more kept coming. For forty five minutes the carriages filled to overflowing, corridors resembling a wartime troop train, bodies and baggage piled everywhere, each compartment bulging, each overhead luggage rack sagging with bodies. Everybody wanted to be on the first train out, not wait around raw and exposed for any others. When the train finally juddered into life it drew a thin cheer, before clanking forward out of Jette station and leaving the scene of the nightmare behind. City gradually gave way to country as the train headed north-west, through the night and through a sleeping Belgium that had just played host to a nightmare. The physical distancing from the scene of the disaster produced a cocktail of indescribable relief and utter exhaustion. We barely spoke, each wrestling with his own thoughts.

A squeal of brakes and the train began its approach into Ostend station, more than three hours later than we should have arrived. And the reception awaiting us showed that this night was far from over.

CHAPTER 8
BACK IN OSTEND

Thursday May 30th 1985: 2am – late afternoon

As our train drew into Ostend station, a solid phalanx of armed police stretched along the entire length of the platform, several deep.

The police presence was massive, overwhelming, intimidating and to us, grotesquely disproportionate, utterly misjudging the mood. In the sheer numbers and their grim and determined demeanour, the police message was clear: zero tolerance. There will be no further disruption in this country tonight.

There wasn't going to be anyway.

As they began leaving the train, the fans stared in bewilderment at the massed uniformed ranks, almost as many on the platform as there were on the train. Our own personal bodyguard. One-to-one care. The barking of countless tethered Alsatian dogs echoed eerily and unnervingly around the station concourse. The only other sound was the slamming of train doors.

Beyond the police ranks we could see the cameras, equipment and searing lights of a British TV news crew, suddenly galvanised into action for the moment it had been waiting for; the arrival of this bedraggled army of killers.

Well, surprisingly enough, no-one seemed in the market for glorifying in infamy or in the mood to discuss the matter. It felt like a sick intrusion, a vile violation into something intensely private, personal and still red raw. Together with the massive police presence, it amounted to too much for a few, and produced a sudden whirlwind of vitriol. A furious tirade pierced the tense unnatural calm of the stand-off: "You fucking sick perverts, what the fuck are you here for, there's nothing to see". "Want to see what a murderer looks like do you, you shitbags?" "Fucking vultures, fuck off home."

At the first raised voices several of the police drew batons and headed straight towards the crowd in a no-nonsense show of machismo, a striking — literally — contrast to the earlier inertia of their Brussels counterparts. Now, too late, when it didn't matter. In normal circumstances this swift and brutal intervention and the presence of the TV news crew would have provoked a riot. Now they drew only meek resignation and angry muttering from Liverpool's tired, dazed, traumatised supporters. There was no stomach for a fight, no stomach for anything apart from going home. We just stood there in simmering resignation, waiting to be herded towards the waiting ferry ... except we didn't want the ferry, we wanted our rooms in Ostend, which lay just the wrong side of a ten-deep mass of police just looking for any excuse ....

Apprehensively, we made our move, breaking away from the stream of fans and headed towards the police cordon. Immediately half a dozen armed officers started moving towards us to quell this insurrection, in a manner you could easily call confrontational. Before they could shove us back from whence we came, we began pleading, hands to our sides in submission and subservience, that we had rooms in Ostend, that our money and passports were there (they weren't — we had them with us, we're not that stupid). The reaction lay somewhere between scepticism and outright aggression. They gave every impression that they did not want to hear another single word of English that night. But following a brief meeting with a senior officer who had come over to see what this mini break-out was about, they decided this was not some ruse to allow us to continue indulging our insatiable bloodlust for a few more hours. Perhaps the thought of not being able to get us out of the country without our passports was the key.

"Where is your hotel?"

"What is the name of your hotel?"

"What street is your hotel in?"

Our pass rate was poor, as our rooms didn't really have names, they were just doorways off side streets with steps leading upstairs, and we had no idea of the streets' names, only how to get to them. Ever tried pronouncing Flemish street names? It'll never catch on as a hobby.

On the other hand, saying "Haven't got a clue mate", whilst being entirely accurate, might not have been to our best advantage. So we quickly invented 'Hotel Atlantic's and 'Rene's' and 'Wilhelmstraats' and tried to sound vague, guessing that their knowledge of the town's lower-end bed-and-breakfast market might be less than encyclopaedic. It would only take one of them to say 'There's no such street as Wilhelmstraat' and the game would be up. Cell time, and probably the business end of a baton. But it seemed to work; after a few seconds of very tense silence, they reluctantly parted to let us through, along with a few others who were in the same situation. In all, maybe 40 or 50 emerged from the station, with huge relief. Outside, the streets were unrecognisable from the brash, noisy neon playground we had been cavorting in less than twenty four hours earlier. Already it seemed part of another life. Windows were shuttered, doors closed; the only light the neat symmetrical orange lines of street lighting. Bars and restaurants closed, streets deserted apart from yet more baton-fingering police and dogs, on every corner, at every junction, and with the same confrontational approach and barely concealed contempt: "You! English! What are you doing here? Where are you going? What is the name of your hotel? Go — NOW!"

But, drained and exhausted, we were beyond provocation. We were now in the early hours of Thursday, and our last proper night's sleep had been Sunday. All we wanted was to put an end to this wretched day. We finally reached our respective accommodations, and arranged to meet the next morning. I suddenly realised how hungry I was; we hadn't eaten for ten hours. But exhaustion overpowered hunger. As I switched off the light and my head hit the pillow, with sleep only a matter of seconds away, I heard Vince's voice through the darkness: "This is probably the last time we'll ever do this, watching Liverpool in a European final."

Not true, as it happened. But we knew Liverpool would now inevitably face a lengthy ban, possibly a permanent one, for its part in what had just happened — even though we were still unclear exactly what that was. That some people had died was now beyond doubt, and that fact alone placed Heysel in a category all of its own. We would now be barred from an experience that we had shared many times and derived incalculable pleasure from. Part of our shared past, and until now part of our shared future. Somehow, even against the enormity of what had just happened, it just didn't seem fair.

It was mid-morning before we awoke. There is that fleeting moment as you wake up, before brute reality kicks your door down, like waking on a Monday morning momentarily convinced it's still Sunday, when yesterday doesn't exist. Did that really happen last night? Did we really go to a European

Cup Final where people died? Another fine sunny morning, one that at any other time would make you feel good, only added to the sense of unreality and dislocation, contrasting so vividly with the deep darkness and despondency that had fallen inside each of us.

We showered, dressed and packed, each still locked in his own private thoughts. It was a sombre, morose band that went to find the owner to pay. We found him in the kitchen. He spun round sharply. The questioning, the suspicion, were in his eyes, his demeanour: "Were you one of them?" Well for all he knew, we may have been; ringleaders in the disaster that had shaken his nation and was dominating world news that morning. Or were we just hyper-sensitive? We paid him and thanked him for the rooms, feeling uncomfortable, ashamed, as though we had somehow let him down and betrayed his trust. "What happened boys?" he asked sadly. We could not answer him, just shrugged shoulders, shook our heads and mumbled vagaries and platitudes. All we had done was follow our football team to the European Cup Final. As individuals we were utterly blameless, so why should we feel apologetic, guilty, almost criminal?

Where is the divide between individual innocence and collective responsibility? When you follow your club, do you do so as an individual, representing only yourself, or as a member of your immediate small group, accountable only for the eight of you (in our case), or are you a representative of the whole body of Liverpool supporters? I knew I was innocent, and I knew all our group was. I knew a huge majority of the Liverpool supporters were too. But I knew that a few beyond our group weren't. How much responsibility does that mean you take on personally? Over the days and weeks to follow, this issue kept bubbling to the surface of the swirling emotional morass. The trouble is, you don't have any precedent to guide you over something as enormous as this. There's nothing to draw on to help you, to show you how you should think and feel and behave. You just have to make it up yourself, and it's hard, really hard. If something amusing happens or is said, are you allowed to laugh? If someone sees you laughing, do they think 'Look, these callous murderers aren't even bothered!' When is it OK to laugh again?

By 11.30am, our full party had reunited by Ostend's bustling harbour, which was about its busy business on another normal working day. The bleary-eyed bewilderment, exhaustion and disarray of our retreat from Brussels just a few hours earlier had undergone a remarkable transformation, at least physically. Our almost cherubic appearance was testimony to the restorative powers of sleep, a shower and some breakfast. In the chaos and confusion, in the urgent flight away from the Heysel Stadium and out of Brussels, we had still not had a chance to let people at home know we were safe in those pre-mobile phone days. Getting away safely had been sole priority, telling people about it would have to wait. Our families would have been on the receiving end of a relentless bombardment of grisly footage and grim statistics, harrowing interviews, post-mortems, emergency telephone numbers and constantly updated fatality and casualty figures. By now they almost certainly knew a great deal more than we did. We took over the row of telephone kiosks by the quayside fishmarket to make some calls. I knew the only way I could speak to my wife that day would be to have a message broadcast at Old Trafford cricket ground, where she was with friends at the England-Australia One Day International. Instead I called my parents; it was one of my brothers who answered.

"Hello Ian."

"Alright mate?" he replied, calmly. He's not the emotional gushing sort. Only gets phased if he breaks a string on his bass.

"Yeah, we're OK. Just about. Tell mum and dad we're OK will you? We're in Ostend now, we'll be back home about midnight tonight."

"Will do. Bit of a sickener last night wasn't it?"

"Could say that. I'll fill in you later. See you."

Already I felt a sense of futility trying to explain how it felt to anyone who hadn't been there. I still do. They will be forever consigned to being outsiders to our dark shared nightmare, and for some considerable time — days and weeks — we would only want to be with others who'd shared it. Jews and Gentiles. As I stepped from the kiosk I glanced at the boats bobbing gently in the calm, glinting water, a stark contrast to the wildly swirling turmoil inside. Could it really have happened only last night, such a small number of hours ago, here in this same country, in this same life?

With the ferry not due until 2pm, we planned to walk into town, buy some newspapers and get some lunch and a beer. With some trepidation, we entered the newsagents; we knew this was going to be tough. Every newspaper in every language, in German, French, Dutch and Flemish as well as English, told the universal story in words and awful photographs, all over their front pages. "*Panique au Heysel*", "*Tragedie en Brosselen*". A French language newspaper carried a horrifically vivid photograph across a double-page spread sparing no detail; one victim could clearly be seen with a dark patch spreading from the crotch of his jeans where the life had literally been crushed out of him. Another could be seen pulling frantically and desperately at an obviously-lifeless corpse, buried beneath a pile of bodies. Bodies draped in a giant Juventus flag were stacked outside the ground by the turnstiles, at the very spot we had passed just minutes before that photograph must have been taken, where the crazed

Italian fans had come charging towards us. Expressions on the faces told the story; the living disbelief and powerlessness, the dead panic and terror, frozen in eternity. The images were unnerving, chilling, shocking, and we just stood and gazed, horrifically transfixed by the coverage.

For some reason, seeing it like this in the newspapers seemed to make it more real than actually being there, 50 metres away, and watching it all unfold. Perhaps we have become so accustomed to receiving our news via the media that we can't recognise reality before it has passed through the media filter. We kept returning to those agonising, stomach-churning photographs, which set off a confusing melee of revulsion and yet compulsion to continue. To the staff and other customers who came into the shop, it must have looked as though we had come to wallow in our handiwork and gloat over our glorious triumph. It wasn't hard to detect the palpable sense of unease at our presence. But they too had a far greater knowledge of events than we had. We needed to catch up fast. We bought every newspaper they had for sale and wandered off down the street, noses buried in our selection of newspapers in different languages, looking like a curiously erudite bunch. Or a disturbingly ghoulish one. There was so much to say, yet so little being said. Sometimes words seem lightweight, inadequate, futile.

The way it was described, what were initially routine terrace scuffles quickly escalated into a series of serious terrace battles. The Liverpool fans had charged into the Juventus supporters, who were hemmed in on three sides by crumbling concrete walls. The Juventus supporters attempted to fall back. However, with no avenue of retreat, they simply piled on top of each other. Panic set in among the Italians, some of whom were now starting to be crushed at the rear of the terrace as the Liverpool supporters continued to charge against the front. At this moment, with police and stewards failing to react, a wall at the Eastern end of the terrace gave way. Dozens of Juventus supporters were now trapped against what remained of the wall, and were trampled underfoot as thousands of people stampeded over them.

Everywhere we went, we could see how much the cautious but trusting welcome of Tuesday had been replaced by blank incomprehension, fear and occasionally ill-concealed disgust. Bars and cafés were suddenly 'closed', 'full' or simply 'not serving'. Yet we were the same eight people who had been welcomed on Tuesday, and had personally done nothing wrong since. We had to try more than half a dozen apparently-open places before finding one that was grudgingly prepared to serve us, and ordered a round of beers and something to eat.

In deep introspection, my thoughts turned from what lay just behind to what now lay ahead for us, both individually and as a close-knit group that went back a long way. How would this affect us? Would we all react the same? Would any decide to stop going to the match? Had the dynamics been altered? And how about when we got home? How would it affect relationships with spouses and family? How could we adjust from this extraordinary experience to the resumption of everyday life and work? How could we re-integrate from this absurd abnormality to the mundane?

I remember once reading that the reason for Keith Moon's notorious bouts of post-gig room-trashing and driving cars into hotel swimming pools was that he just couldn't cope with the contrast between the incredible high of The Who's stage shows and the flat featureless ordinariness that came when they were over. How would we cope with our own crashing come-down?

Moreover, it wasn't just a question of how we would handle

it in the days and weeks to come, but how other people would. There would be the inevitable battery of questions that I didn't want to deal with, over and over. If you get tired of answering: "How was your weekend/holiday/Christmas?", how much worse would this be? How many times would we be asked to retell the story, whilst not wanting to? If only you could insert an answer message with your stock reply on it, and just press the button. There would be bland, inadequate platitudes as people sought to gloss over or trivialise it. There would be those who just ignored it and pretended it hadn't happened. That wouldn't go down very well either — something fundamental to me has just happened and you just ignore it? Worse still, there would be the wind-ups, the judgments and accusations, the cheap jokes, you just knew it. Even imagining it made me grow angry. It was going to be very hard for us, but I suppose quite hard for others too. But I wasn't going to be looking at it from their point of view for some time yet.

Then there was the media and the supporters of other football clubs to contend with. We pretty much knew what to expect from the former. From the latter would come torrents of snide comments, relentless taunting, abuse, provocation, recriminations, blame. They all held us solely responsible for the blanket ban imposed on all English clubs from European football in the wake of Heysel. In truth, the supporters of just about every English team that had ever played in European football had all made their own ample contributions to the general poor reputation of English football fans, and most certainly the fans of the England national team had done so. They had spent years huffing and puffing, before Liverpool's fans blew the house down. From UEFA's point of view, Heysel was only the last straw, not the whole edifice.

On one occasion, years later, I recall a man in the main stand at Oxford United (of all places — hardly one of football's hotbeds, nor a place of particular Liverpool antipathy), blaming "Liverpool murderers" for his team's absence from European competition. The reaction he got was, to put it politely, vehement. Phil told him, in terms not normally associated with that university town, that it was like blaming the whole of Yorkshire for the Yorkshire Ripper. To this day, supporters of rival clubs — notably Everton and Manchester United — sing 'Murderers' to Liverpool's supporters. Well there was no murder, no charge of murder. To be more legally and factually accurate, they could amend their chant to 'Manslaughterers, with responsibility shared amongst several other agencies too', but I accept that wouldn't scan very well. And it would still be far too simplistic.

Although the vast majority of Liverpool's supporters had by now left Belgium, we knew there'd still be a few hundred stragglers sharing our ferry journey, those who had missed their scheduled transport after last night's chaos, and those like us who had made their own accommodation arrangements. We knew for certain the bar on the ferry would be closed for the duration — and this time it was — so after lunch we bought some food for the journey and called at an off-licence near the railway station to stock up. If ever I am in Belgium there is a standing order to bring home a few of their vast selection of supreme bottled beers, mostly for myself but also my brother, so I stocked up with a few including some Duvels, using up what few Belgian francs we had left. With our supplies stuffed into holdalls, travel bags and polythene carrier bags, we clanked down the street towards the ferry terminal.

Despite the absence of team colours or any other external

displays of allegiance to a football team, it was obvious we were all Liverpool fans, therefore had forfeited any entitlement to decent or civilised treatment. That at any rate was how the large police contingent at the port entrance clearly saw it. They were stopping, questioning and searching most English people and all who looked like they just might be football fans. As those two groups made up almost the entire complement of passengers, the process was proving time-consuming and cumbersome. We had assumed they would want us out of the country as quickly as possible — a desire we shared entirely. When my turn finally came to be vetted and scrutinised, my bulging, clanking polythene bag attracted instant attention. A policeman peered inside and seized my precious cargo, just confiscated it without explanation or eye contact, and placed the bag behind him to join a vast mountain — or perhaps lake — of similarly confiscated booze. Mark joined me in the record books in the "Shortest time in possession of a four pack" category. Quickly sizing up what was happening just ahead of them, Phil, Don and the others took advantage of the distraction to hastily repack their beer into their holdalls and slip through unchallenged, despite the giveaway clanking. Mark and I began to protest about this state-sponsored theft and infringement of civil rights, but judging by the reaction, we were teetering on the brink of a short spell of Belgian residency. This was not the moment for a civil liberties campaign.

"Don't worry, we'll have a party when you've gone," growled one of the policemen.

Deep below, the engines rumbled into life, and the ferry slid slowly away from Ostend dock to bring to an end this tumultuous time in Belgium. I watched its coastline slowly recede, wondering how long (if ever) it would be before we would be making another trip like this to follow Liverpool.

After twenty continuous, virtually trouble-free years in Europe, it felt like our first major transgression would be our last.

Downstairs by the luggage hold we saw the guy who had been stabbed in the leg by the hot-dog vendor before the match, lying against the wall. He wasn't easy to miss, with a huge dried bloodstain still caked over his jeans. As he sat in the ambulance that sped him to hospital yesterday, sirens wailing, he could have been forgiven for thinking that he was the one making the news, not knowing that his own micro-tragedy was about to be totally eclipsed.

Don had already found himself a place on the top deck and surrounded himself with all the paraphernalia of the sun zealot — deck chair, sunglasses and some see-through plastic flip-flops, which allow for foot-tanning, apparently. The rest of us could easily live with the stigma of having untanned feet. As the bars were clearly going to remain firmly shut, we followed on up to the sun deck, joining many Liverpool supporters basking under more cloudless blue sky, which made what happened only last night seem a surreal and ugly intrusion.

CHAPTER 9
WELCOME HOME

Thursday May 30th – Friday May 31st, 1985.

A few hundred supporters piled onto the train to take us from Victoria Station to Euston and the last leg of our journey home. This meant sharing the escalators and corridors with an entirely separate community, the capital's commuters, each with no part in the others' world, passing each other without acknowledgment, eyes averted save for the odd furtive glance. It felt like being in some oversized identity parade.

The oppressive silence was shattered by a lone hysterical female shriek from somewhere above on the escalator: "Murderers!" In an instant, tension turned into fury, and a ferocious verbal bombardment echoed around the Underground's honeycomb of chambers: "Keep your fuckin' trap shut girl, you know fuck all." All the other commuters looked around sharply and nervously. If you had just arrived at the scene at that precise moment, and just heard the abuse but not the reason for it, all you'd have witnessed was a savage, foul-mouthed, unprovoked tirade at an innocent girl.

You'd have shaken your head in disbelief at these shameless louts who just didn't know when to stop. You'd go on to tell your fellow travellers and families and friends and work colleagues about the disgusting spectacle you had witnessed, perpetrated by that same worthless bunch we saw on the TV last night. You'd have had all your prejudices reinforced, and would have revelled in having been proved right all along; yes, they really are as bad as they're presented.

In this way the stereotypes harden, the entrenchment deepens, and from our perspective, a lingering sense of injustice festered at the sheer, impenetrable edifice of closed-minded condemnation we had to face. Having left these shores, just a few days yet a lifetime ago, with such hopes, such pride, we were about to find out what it feels like to be despised and reviled in our own country. We were victims of Heysel too, we were suffering from it. It would have been very comforting to run into a little compassion and understanding.

At Euston many fans used the phones to call home, and Phil returned fuming from his call: his wife had been pestered by the local newspaper, which had somehow uncovered a 'Local Man in Heysel Riot' story and despatched someone to hang around his house all day. It was an aspect we hadn't even considered; but living where we did, in small-ish provincial towns in the Midlands, our story would be local news, unlike on Merseyside where you'd expect half the population to be at the match. It would be easy enough for a local newspaper to trace us; our support for Liverpool and our presence at Heysel was known by enough people within our own communities, it wouldn't take a resourceful hack long.

After the TV crew at Ostend station, the attitude of police and civilians in Ostend and the reaction of the public in London, now we had this unwarranted intrusion to contend with. It felt sickening that local rags might try to make capital out of Heysel, intruding on private grief of which they had no conception. We felt very weary and worn down, and just wanted to be home. As we boarded the Birmingham train for a journey that seemed to last forever, we agreed that any co-operation with any media requests would be only on condition that no photographs be used — we did not seek personal publicity or notoriety, and did not want to be presented as such — and that the newspaper agreed to make a donation to any Heysel appeal fund that would inevitably follow. That would probably be enough to deter most local newspapers.

We walked out of Birmingham New Street station just after midnight. Owing to the lateness of the ferry and subsequent connections, we had just missed our last train home. We were in no mood for one more hurdle, but Phil, as a railway employee, knew about their responsibility to get you home in such circumstances. We headed for the Manager's office, and to his credit and our gratitude, he ordered us a taxi, without charge, for the 40-mile round trip. One by one we were dropped off, having arranged to meet in the pub the following lunchtime. I was last drop. The taxi bumped into the familiar cul-de-sac on a sleeping housing estate. I thanked the driver, not least for not trying to charge me the astronomical figure on the meter, and got out. A passing insomniac out walking his dog spoke: "I didn't know anywhere was open this time of night."

"There isn't. Actually I just got back from the match in Belgium", I muttered wearily.

"Oh" he said blankly, and sauntered off.

My wife was in bed, but awake.

"I wasn't worried", she said. "Why should I have been worried? Anyone could see it wasn't Liverpool's section where the wall went."

Bloody near it though. Besides, you didn't have to die at Heysel to be affected by it. But that's how my wife dealt with it, with life generally. Reductionist.

"Oh, right," was all I could muster. Remember that compassion I was talking about? She's not my wife now.

But for then, the rest would keep. I had to sleep.

Friday May 31st, 1985.

When I finally awoke, my wife had long since left for work, but had left all yesterday's newspapers for me. It's part of the ground rules when you're away for a big game — set the video, order the newspapers. It's your chance to relive the sweetest of moments and extend the euphoria a little longer, or alternatively to trawl through your private grief for clues as to how it went wrong and why you lost. You'd hate to get back from your great triumph and have no record of it. Yesterday's newspapers, and today's poking through the letterbox, were in their way just as compelling as if they had been celebratory, and I pored over them in some sort of morbid post-trauma addiction, hunting for an angle I might have missed, a crumb, a tiny detail, something that might begin to unscramble the tangle for me. It didn't, of course. But having existed so far largely on a diet of hearsay and rumour, we all felt an insatiable desire for facts, and through them, comprehension. And perhaps even mitigation.

Inevitably, Heysel coverage totally dominated the newspapers, and it wasn't hard to summarise the tone: a raging torrent of spite, bile and hysteria, fire and brimstone of biblical proportions and enough humbug to choke on. One headline after another called for the banning of Liverpool and all English clubs from European competition, even for the banning of football itself (does that make them *banner* headlines?), until it/they "got their house in order", whatever that meant. Fleet Street thesauruses had been worked to a pulp by the red tops to find variations on "scum", "thugs" and "punish". From their screaming headlines, from leader comments and from readers' letters, from the football authorities, commentators, observers, the government and the public, the message was universal, the verdict unanimous: *guilty*. No redeeming or mitigating factors. Guilty. We — Liverpool supporters — must be made an example of and receive the sternest punishment.

To someone who had actually been there, it felt maddeningly, infuriatingly mono-dimensional and incomplete. A complex concurrence of circumstances had been reduced to child-like simplicity, and I just couldn't reconcile what I was reading with what I had experienced. Besides, taking a lecture on morality, ethics and standards of behaviour from Thatcher's government (in my eyes a truly malevolent influence on the very fabric of British life) and its baying, sycophantic lackeys in the British press amounted to a greater dosage of hypocrisy than I could stomach. What gave these people the right to vilify me for being a Liverpool supporter who had been at Heysel yet committed no offence? Furious, frustrated and nauseated, I turned to the video. I watched some charging across the terraces, some shadow boxing and air-flailing between fans across the fence. I watched the Belgian authorities' feeble attempts to restore order, the interminable delay, the shocked commentary, more over-simplification by 'experts', more blanket condemnation of the same supporters, the same people, who once earned so much praise and respect, who had been a credit to their country in Paris and Rome, who had for twenty years been ambassadors of English football on the continent, welcomed rather than feared. Fifteen minutes of anomaly could erase all those hard-earned years of goodwill, just like that? Without anybody pausing to ask how and why something so out of character might have happened? They didn't even realise that it *was* out of character.

The video confirmed that Juventus probably shouldn't have been awarded the penalty that won the match, and that Liverpool probably should have had one, but who cared? The game, devoid of quality and bereft of relevance, was not worth keeping, and I didn't need a documentary record of the rest. I wiped the tape, and set off to meet the others at lunchtime, as arranged. Normal life would have to reassert itself soon enough — not least with work the following Monday — but not yet.

At the pub we were ready to talk, as long as it was only about Heysel, and we talked and talked, a released torrent. We talked about how difficult it was, and was going to be, to readjust to everyday life, about our reluctance to let anything or anyone else into our lives, about how anything not related to Heysel seemed irrelevant, pointless, an unwelcome intrusion, about how hard it was to properly absorb the enormity of what had occurred, about individual innocence and collective responsibility. Feelings remained elusively, frustratingly muddy, unformed, intangible, like trying to plait candyfloss. Many knots still needed teasing out.

We also talked about the prospects for Liverpool Football Club and its supporters, about how we as supporters might be affected when following Liverpool post-Heysel. The prevailing mood was, unsurprisingly, very pessimistic. A lengthy ban from European football was inevitable, depriving the club not only of a significant source of its income but a major source of its prestige and inspiration. The club's top players would surely be lured away for European football with other clubs, either other English clubs (at this point, the decision to ban not only Liverpool but all English clubs had not yet been announced) or European ones, and quality replacements would be difficult to attract for the same reason. Attendances, already reduced by the absence of those who had vowed, post-Heysel, never to watch football again, would drop further with the exodus of top players, declining playing standards, a growing inability to compete and the missing glitter and incentive of European involvement. The heart, it seemed, had been ripped out of the club. There was no alternative, it seemed, to an inescapable spiral of decline. It felt as though we did actually, after all, know one casualty at Heysel, and that was Liverpool Football Club itself. In that immediate aftermath it felt as though our precious club's reputation lay mangled amidst the rubble of Z block.

There was a more positive counter-argument. A new manager, Kop idol Kenny Dalglish, had been appointed post-Heysel after the devastated incumbent, Joe Fagan, stood down. Would not the team and its new manager need our support like never before? Would we desert the club in its hour of greatest need, or unite behind it? Would staying away just be handing victory to the hooligans, the media, the government, the Liverpool-haters?

But we knew that the whole business of following Liverpool Football Club had changed. Where once we had swaggered, we would now be expected to slink. Where once we felt pride, now we would have to contend with guilt and shame. We would — had already — face abuse and hatred. Almost overnight, the club and we, its followers, had descended from much that's good about football and football supporters to becoming synonymous with all that was wrong with it, at home and abroad.

Ultimately, and with the help of a few beers, we decided that we would still be there for the first home game of the coming season, our first competitive match post-Heysel and what would surely be one of the most testing of occasions. In fact, attendances at Anfield actually increased after Heysel, as if it had proved a rallying point. Our fears on the playing front also proved groundless, as the very next season saw Liverpool win the league championship/FA Cup double for the first time in the club's history, and they were only denied it twice more by the last game of two more seasons: in 1988 by losing the FA Cup Final to Wimbledon; and in 1989 by losing the league title to Arsenal with only seconds left. During that late '80s period after Heysel, Liverpool produced a quality of football that even we had rarely encountered before. In all the club went on to win the league three times and the FA Cup twice in the five seasons after Heysel. At home at least, normal service was resumed. But Heysel's wound bit deep. It was only another, statistically greater disaster, at Hillsborough less than four years later, that pushed the pain of Heysel out of our collective psyche.

We are still accused of valuing our own supporters' lives ahead of those who died at Heysel, of forgetting them in our quest for Hillsborough justice. But they are separate events, separate tragedies with different circumstances, there's no linkage. Wanting justice from Hillsborough doesn't mean you dismiss Heysel. There's room to care about both.

But one supplanted the other because it happened later, and it happened to our own people, and on a purely statistical level, it was a far greater tragedy. Also, at Hillsborough, Liverpool's supporters were entirely blameless, an argument we couldn't use at Heysel.

CHAPTER 10
IN CONCLUSION

In the days and weeks that followed, Heysel continued to dominate the news. From the newspapers to TV chat shows to the House of Commons, it was just about the only topic of debate. A few days later, British Prime Minister Margaret Thatcher pressured the FA to ban all English clubs from Europe indefinitely. Our own Football Association had pre-empted them by withdrawing our clubs from the following season's European tournaments pending UEFA's announcements. Two days later she was granted her wish as UEFA banned all English sides for what they stated was "an indeterminate period of time". Liverpool received an additional ban of "indeterminate plus three years", or more precisely, three further years in which Liverpool qualified for European competition. If they didn't, the ban would roll on until they did. Given Thatcher's previously stated dislike of the city of Liverpool — probably because of its left-wing politics and strong opposition to her government and philosophy — and her very apparent dislike of football and football supporters generally, we hardly expected any help from her. It was the excuse she and her cronies had been looking for to put the boot into football just the way they had with the miners.

She and the Queen issued formal apologies to the people of Belgium and Italy. That must have helped. Liverpool Football Club itself would have been justified in feeling harshly treated; it had done all within its powers to control its own supporters, and sold no tickets for the ill-fated Block Z. It was not the club's fault that some other agency fatally did so, nor that some of its supporters could not resist a punch-up. Liverpool FC also had no part in the decision to stage a major match at Heysel in the first place; indeed Liverpool's secretary Peter Robinson urgently requested that UEFA move the final to a more suitable and safer venue, but his plea was ignored. Neither was the club responsible for the appalling condition of the Heysel Stadium, the inadequate supervision outside it or the supine inertia of the authorities inside it. Above all, Liverpool FC had good reason, based on precedent, to trust its supporters.

In the end, the ban on English clubs competing in Europe ran for five years, with Liverpool's extra three years reduced by two. As English clubs had dominated the European Cup in the eight seasons before Heysel, winning it seven times (Liverpool in 1977 , 1978, 1981 and 1984, Nottingham Forest in 1979 and 1980, and Aston Villa in 1982), this left a considerable hole in Europe's most prestigious football competition. It took until 1999 for an English club to win it again, with Manchester United's victory in Barcelona. That long gap was Liverpool's fault too, apparently, because all our clubs had to catch up again after the ban that Liverpool caused.

So Liverpool's "punishment" was only an extra season's ban beyond that of the other English clubs that qualified for European football. But in truth the ban was the bill English football had to pay not only for Heysel but for over a decade of violence by English football followers, in which Liverpool's supporters actually played very little part. Incomprehensibly, the English national team, the epicentre of more exported hooliganism than all the individual clubs put together, was never banned, and was still allowed to participate in international football in Europe. So the very same fans, the very same individuals, whose clubs were banned had only to trade their club colours for their country to be able to roam the continent freely and legitimately following England. The inconsistency of UEFA's decisions extended to the remarkable leniency shown to Juventus for the considerable part played by their supporters in the disturbances at Heysel. Their "punishment" was to begin the defence of the trophy they won in Brussels by playing their home European Cup games the following season behind closed doors. Hardly hard line. The point was made that Juventus' fans had no particular 'previous' before Heysel; true, but neither did Liverpool's.

But such was the prevailing terrace culture of the mid-'80s, with violence endemic in and around football grounds throughout England, and such was the level of antagonism surrounding English football at the time, that a major crowd disaster was bound to happen somewhere, sometime. In *Fever Pitch*, Nick Hornby puts it this way:

'The kids' stuff that proved murderous in Brussels belonged firmly and clearly on a continuum of apparently harmless but obviously threatening acts — violent chants, wanker signs, the whole, petty hardact works — in which a very large minority of fans had been indulging for nearly 20 years. In short Heysel was an organic part of a culture that many of us, myself included, had contributed towards.'

A series of goodwill gestures and well-intentioned wound dressing between the two clubs and cities followed — memorial services in Liverpool and Turin, exchange visits between the two cities, the possibility of a friendly match in Turin between the clubs. British and Belgian police forces swapped intelligence and photographs ad infinitum — you couldn't pick up a newspaper or switch on the TV without seeing a circled "wanted" face. The Belgian government creaked under the weight of questioning and accusations of gross incompetence, and, fatally holed below the waterline, eventually sank. Meanwhile its British counterpart, Thatcher's hang 'em flog 'em brigade, maintained a continuous stream of anti-football, anti-Liverpool invective, threatening draconian crowd control measures, the introduction of identity cards and probably the reintroduction of National Service and the death penalty, the compulsory sterilisation of Liverpool mothers or the ritual slaughter of their first-born. Scapegoats were in huge demand, and the slavering tabloid press led the hunt voraciously, revelling in its self-appointed role as the Voice of Reason whilst displaying absolutely none, and the licence Heysel appeared to give it to rant unchecked in an orgy of self-righteous bigotry. Balance and reason, it seemed, had no part in this public "debate".

A series of increasingly bizarre and surreal conspiracy theories began to emerge in the wake of Heysel; there were reports of extremist right-wing groups having been present, claims that swastika flags and banners and far-right propaganda had been found amongst the debris. There were some suggestions that these may have belonged not to British but Italian fascists who had been there to agitate. It would certainly be difficult to imagine stonier ground for right-wing dogma than the vast bulk of Liverpool supporters, whose red allegiance was not confined to football. Their politics, and the city they come from, inclined sharply towards the left.

The very day after the disaster, UEFA's chief observer,

Gunter Schneider, stated, "Only the English fans were responsible. Of that there is no doubt." He said 'English' fans, not solely Liverpool fans, because several Juventus supporters who were at the game had claimed that there were supporters from many British clubs, including Chelsea. Not quite as unfeasible as it may sound; Chelsea stood to gain from a Liverpool victory — or a Liverpool ban — as they themselves would then qualify for European football the following season. Besides, a European Cup Final in Brussels would make an attractive, possibilities-packed Bank Holiday week alternative for a Londoner, just a short and easy hop across the water and barely further than Brighton, Southend or Margate.

The lack of ticket control at the ground certainly made it impossible for the authorities to know who was in the ground and where; here's an account from a football website — though not a Liverpool one:

"It was impossible for police to weed out known troublemakers, and easy for pockets of hard core hooligans to assemble wherever they wished. As a result, two hours before kick off, perhaps the most malevolent assembly of football supporters ever seen in one place had gathered, and as far as they were concerned, it was payback time (for Rome 1984). It should be understood that not just Liverpool hooligans were present. There were contingents from a great many firms all over the country, from Luton MIGS to Millwall Bushwackers, West Ham ICF and Newcastle Toon Army. After the events in Rome, club rivalries had been put aside: Juventus were to catch the full fury of the English hooligan elite. There was a score to settle."

The Heysel disaster's capacity to fire the imagination reached its nadir when, in April 1986, nearly a year later, a typed, unsigned letter bearing a Los Angeles postmark was received by *The Guardian* newspaper in London, claiming that the whole tragedy of Heysel had been a "mafia-inspired conspiracy" to blacken the name of soccer and so further the worldwide expansion of American football. "Italian Americans," it said, "mingled with the Juventus supporters to provoke trouble; Liverpool fans, and English soccer in general, took the rap." Well the last bit was undeniable; but the theory sounded more like a plot for a paperback and the product of an over-fertile imagination.

All I can say is that none of these things were witnessed by any of us. Although it did not feel quite like the usual Liverpool crowd that fateful evening in Brussels, and much as though we would love to be able to shed some of the responsibility and have it shared by Chelsea or any other club's fans, right-wing extremists or the Mafia, the fact is that when twenty six names to be charged with manslaughter were released, most had Merseyside addresses.

The release of those names triggered a protracted period of legal jousting and bumbling as the process leading to their extradition degenerated towards farce. It wasn't until late in 1987 that the accused were finally taken to Belgium to face trial, after over two years of waiting to have their fates decided. It seemed that everything connected to the Heysel, even afterwards, had to be tainted by incompetence.

The 'Official Reports' season duly began. Firstly, the Popplewell Report on crowd safety and control at sports grounds, already commissioned by the UK Government pre-Heysel, had its remit widened to incorporate a specific study of Heysel. Published in January 1986, it acknowledged that the first crowd disturbances at Heysel had in fact occurred at the other end, where the main body of Juventus supporters stood, as they clashed with police. This, the report stated, led to English fans firing flares and throwing stones into the mostly-Italian crowd in Block Z — an observation so at odds with what the ranters in Government and media preferred to believe that they ignored it completely. The report went on:

"Between 7.15 and 7.30pm, English fans charged Block Z. There were three charges, the third resulted in the Italian supporters in Block Z, who were seeking to escape, being squashed and suffocated. Everyone knows that those guilty of the violence, those responsible for the deaths of the victims, are the violent groups amongst the English supporters."

The report acknowledged the poor condition of the stadium and the failure of the police to intervene quickly enough or take adequate action, and added, with masterly understatement, that "a ban on the sale of alcohol outside the ground was not enforced". Indeed it wasn't.

By November 1986, after an 18-month investigation, the dossier of top Belgian judge Mrs Marina Coppieters was finally published. In sharp contrast to the one-sided version of events on this side of the Channel, it concluded that perhaps blame should not rest solely with the English fans, but instead should be shared by the police and football authorities. Several top officials were incriminated by some of the dossier's findings, including police captain Johan Mahieu, who had been in charge of security on May 29th 1985 and was now charged with involuntary manslaughter.

That bears repeating: *the police captain who had been in charge of security at the Heysel Stadium was charged with involuntary manslaughter.* How many anti-Liverpool ranters over Heysel are aware of that? Then again, many of them weren't even born at the time, but just accepted their own club's fans' warped view of it.

We had known all along that without significant other factors, there would have been no deaths, no major news story, just a minor routine pre-match skirmish followed by a game of football. That somebody somewhere had finally acknowledged it brought huge relief.

There is no doubt that events at Heysel Stadium amounted to a disaster without parallel for European football. Neither the Ibrox or Bradford disasters that preceded it, nor Hillsborough that was to follow, though all involved loss of life, had crowd violence at their core. In football terms they were also purely domestic affairs, with no pan-European dimension.

It has become the accepted version of events that the Heysel stadium disaster was solely the result of hooliganism and rioting by Liverpool fans. Yet none of the 39 victims lost their lives as a result of being beaten, kicked, stoned or stabbed. And none who fought and sought to intimidate and subjugate did so with murder in mind or with even the faintest notion of what was about to follow. Perhaps only an architect or engineer could have foreseen those. Even describing the skirmishes at Heysel as 'rioting' would be misleading. Judged by the standards of the time, or indeed any time, what Heysel actually witnessed was nothing more than a token bout of territorial terrace ritual involving some fist-flailing and air-punching during which few blows were actually landed and from which few injuries resulted. On any other day it would have led to nothing more than the odd bloody nose or black eye, a bit of tut-tutting from onlookers and commentators, with the whole episode of minor scale pre-match disturbance completely forgotten and unreported as soon as the game got underway. Some missiles were thrown — in both directions — and several charges across the terracing occurred. Threatening and unpleasant behaviour, but wholly unexceptional at that time, and only possible because it was made possible. Nowadays it wouldn't be.

But then a wall collapsed and changed everything. Ultimately, what converted an unremarkable skirmish into a fatal tragedy, what transported Heysel from the mundane to the extraordinary, was not the scale or degree of savagery but decaying cement, a structural defect, the final executioner not hooligans but the crumbling, decomposing perimeter wall of Block Z. The wall, no more than four feet high and twenty feet long, was more than 50 years old, its cement cladding crumbling away from the rotting brickwork. Its obscene result was 39 fatalities.

Hooliganism was only the penultimate link in a long chain that stretched right back to our first sight of the match ticket, in that Coventry pub on a Monday evening a full nine days before the match, when we first saw that portentous blob overprinted across the letter Z. To us, it clearly signified that Block Z would be either empty or occupied by neutrals, for crowd segregation purposes. That's how it always was in England and Europe at the time, for every single game, with rival fans segregated and empty buffer zones between them.

But instead, 5,000 supposedly "neutral" tickets for Block Z were placed on open sale in Brussels. On the morning of the day that they went on sale, they were all gone. Inevitably and utterly predictably, most found their way towards Brussels' substantial local Italian population or to Juventus supporters back in Italy, after large blocks of tickets had been bought up by Italian travel agents and ticket touts, with very few falling into neutral local Belgian hands. The open sale was halted when this became apparent, but too late. They were sold or sold on to the people who were to die. That was the first link in the chain, and when the tragedy of the Heysel Stadium really began. The Belgian football union, which organised the match, had taken the decision to sell those tickets rather than allocate them to the two finalist clubs, to increase its profits from the game. Anyone involved with football would have known what was going to happen to those tickets beforehand, it was blindingly obvious. As the Popplewell Report confirmed:

"... some organisations bought large quantities of tickets ... by using their employees to take it in turns to go to the ticket windows. A large number of tickets for Block Z came into the hands of Juventus fans."

So the stadium management and presumably UEFA and the local police, knew in advance that Block Z, the block immediately adjacent to the main body of Liverpool supporters, would be neither empty nor neutral, but occupied by rival supporters. *They already knew that.* You don't have to be a genius to work out the potential danger of such an arrangement. So wouldn't you reasonably expect, given this advance knowledge, that Block Z would be strongly policed and segregation rigidly enforced? Instead there was no gap at all between the two sets of supporters, no empty buffer zone, and just a flimsy stretch of chest-high chicken wire between them, unable to withstand any attempt to breach it and guaranteed not to deter one. And the police presence in that area of the ground? When the exchanges between the rival sets of fans began, there were "five policemen and two dogs" separating the crowds, which would sound laughable if the consequences hadn't been as they were. Even then, after those initial exchanges, when the potential problems had made themselves all too clear, there was still no response, either from the handful of police present in that area or more tellingly, from the police control (I use the term loosely) operation at the stadium. That would have been the obvious time and opportunity to send in numbers, restore order and separate the two sets of fans with an armed human barrier. It certainly would have happened in England. It later transpired that that the police in Block Z had been poorly trained, strictly third division, 'the bottom of the basket' as the French phrase has it. Nor was there a police command centre in the Heysel Stadium to coordinate response, and besides, police radios weren't working anyway, to compound their inability to react to the situation. Furthermore, the officer in charge of policing had not attended any of the planning meetings before the European Cup Final. In short, the police operation was an utter shambles, which explains why the officer in charge received the involuntary manslaughter charge.

In summary, none of the usual factors to prevent or discourage confrontation was in place. As British police forces responsible for crowd control at English football matches will confirm, these are basic precautions. The control and planning at Heysel fell shamefully short of the most elementary requirements, and amounted to a dereliction of responsibility that made effective crowd segregation impossible. The then secretary of Liverpool FC, Peter Robinson, said:

'From day one I was concerned about this neutral area. I argued all along that we should have one end and Juventus the other. We suggested there should be a meeting between the two clubs but the Belgian authorities said no. There were serious planning mistakes. That doesn't excuse what happened, but the problems would not have occurred if it had been done in a different way. It could all have been avoided.'

Short of withdrawing from the match because of their concerns, there was little more that the club itself could have done either before, during or after Heysel.

Long before the day of the game, many concerns had been expressed that the ground was unsafe. When Arsenal had played there several years previously, their supporters had complained about how dilapidated the stadium was. Built in the 1920s, the Heysel Stadium was quite possibly the worst venue in the world to host such a volatile encounter. The game was due to be the last match ever played at the ground, as it had been condemned many years previously for failing to meet modern standards of safety and design. As a result, little money had been spent upon it, and large parts of the stadium were crumbling.

When ordered by the judge to survey the disaster scene, leading Belgian architect Joseph Ange concluded:

"... areas reserved for standing room [including the ill-fated Block Z] remain as they were at the time of their construction in 1930. They are in an advanced state of decay. Only the hand-rest remains on most of the handrails, most are unstable and several on the point of collapse. The handrails were quickly and easily destroyed by the pressure of the crowds, which had no proper means of escape. Concrete terracing was eroded and, crucially, neither the barrier between Blocks Y and Z nor the wall in Block Z were strong enough to resist crowd pressure."

A London council surveyor sent to the stadium after the tragedy confirmed that there was no way in which it would have been allowed to operate under British regulations. Hans Bangerter, then general secretary for UEFA, criticised the police, though not UEFA themselves of course: "The disaster would not have happened if our specific instructions on security had not been so badly disregarded by the Brussels police and especially the gendarmerie. The English vandals would not have been able to perform such terrible deeds and create such misery if they had not been helped by the frightful incompetence of the Belgian security forces."

Nor if your organisation had selected an appropriate venue in the first place and not ignored advice and even pleas to switch it, Mr. Bangerter.

This article appeared in the *News on Sunday* on July 12 1987:

"I went to the Heysel Stadium in the autumn of 1984 — about six months before the disaster — for a World Cup qualifying match. I remember only too well the reaction of myself and my friends upon entering the stadium; it was an absolute disgrace. Rickety safety barriers, crumbling walls, ancient terracing, non-existent facilities: a recipe for disaster if ever I saw one. Of one thing I am certain; if basic safety checks had been made and proper segregation been enforced, that wall would not have collapsed and those people would still be alive now. That stadium would have been unfit for a women's institute convention, never mind a European Cup Final. And as far as the received wisdom that all the trouble was caused by Liverpool fans — I remember vividly the Italian thugs with their fascist flags and their 'Reds are Animals' banner, the guy with the gun, the stick-throwing mobs ... and above all, I remember the total impotence and incompetence of the Belgian authorities who stood by while a full scale riot took place, completely and utterly unprepared. A number of Englishmen, not all from Liverpool, behaved like evil scum. They should be extradited and dealt with in the severest possible manner by the Belgian authorities. But it is my contention that the blame should be shared by the Italian thugs, and by the Belgians themselves. We should never forget what happened in Brussels. But it's time we threw off the guilt, which is not all ours by any means."

It was also reported that, "... while it is true that the stadium was in abject condition, that Juventus' supporters found their way into a supposedly neutral section at the

Liverpool end, and that local police inflamed the situation, the fact is that without these antagonistic charges, nobody would have died."

Well, you could just as easily turn that around. Had the stadium not been in abject condition, had Juventus' supporters not found their way into a supposedly neutral section at the Liverpool end, had local police not inflamed the situation, nobody would have died either. It took all those factors to be present for the tragedy to occur, you can't just highlight one over another because it suits your purposes.

Yet despite all the concerns about the Heysel Stadium's unsuitability as a venue for a match of such magnitude, and the ticking time bomb of ticket distribution in Section Z, UEFA still refused to amend their decision that this outdated and universally condemned stage was suitable and safe for Europe's showpiece football match between two of Europe's most passionately-followed teams. In doing so they were taking a dangerous and highly irresponsible risk. They gambled and lost, and blamed somebody else.

Poor crowd control and segregation and a stadium in appalling condition is a potentially lethal combination. As a result of the ticket selling arrangements and the decision to overlook the ground's poor condition, 50,000 people were in danger without realising it, before they even left home. These elements were already swirling in the ether long before the day of the game itself; all it would take for the final link in the chain to be joined was a couple of other factors, notably the failure to enforce an alcohol ban and the presence of forged tickets in circulation. It just left the hooligans to deliver the *coup de grâce*.

Nobody from UEFA, European football's governing body, has ever been truly called to account for the tragic events in Brussels, and for their disastrous decision to stage the game at this shambles of a stadium. UEFA has never had the decency to admit to its culpability, to its significant part in what happened. Liverpool's hooligan fringe kept the authorities out of the spotlight where they really belonged, right alongside them.

Over the years, much of the worst of football violence has occurred outside the stadia, in surrounding streets and town centres. Where crowd trouble has occurred inside football grounds, two factors have routinely been present; inadequate crowd segregation and alcohol. By May 1985, there was every reason to expect that the football authorities and police everywhere had learnt those lessons. Alcohol had long been banned inside grounds and on organised transport to matches, and fans had long come to accept that bars near to grounds would be closed. Indeed, finding a bar or pub open and trading normally near a ground would almost be an insult to a hooligan, as though he had been deemed not worthy of special measures, not dangerous enough, his presence not acknowledged, thus providing every motivation to prove them wrong. A town shuttered and boarded up whilst its residents cower behind locked doors and hold their breath is enough to make any hooligan burst with macho pride. It is possible, even commonplace, for a city to impose a fairly effective, if not cast-iron, alcohol curfew. Rome had certainly got close to it twelve months before Heysel. Of course it is an imposition upon the normal lives of the local population, and of course it isn't fair. Of course it cannot be justified just because some English can't control themselves after a few beers. But it can be done.

In Brussels, however, it was harder to find a bar that was closed, even in the vicinity of the Heysel Stadium itself, including one right opposite the main approach to the stadium for Liverpool supporters. We witnessed with rising disbelief (and it must be said, delight) how easy it was to buy beer. For the bars of Brussels it was business as usual, and they did a lot of business that hot sunny day. The carrot was dangled, and taken voraciously. It meant many Liverpool fans arrived in varying stages of intoxication — that is beyond doubt. But there was another, less obvious effect of the bars remaining open: it sent a signal that today lads, all your usual rigorous match day disciplines and impositions are suspended. This cultural remission made it feel like being on holiday; the end of wartime rationing; a prisoner finding his cell door wide open and nobody about. A tone was set, and an underswell of recklessness, lawlessness and anarchy developed: we don't have to behave today. Some football supporters don't need any second invitation, but they got one nonetheless.

If any confirmation was needed that normal rules had been suspended for the day, the casual *laissez faire* attitude of the police and the flimsy security checks outside and inside the ground provided plenty. In another major departure from convention, few fans were stopped and searched at the turnstiles, or had their tickets checked on the approaches to the stadium. In Paris in 1981, fans had been required to show their tickets at several concentric rings of steel before reaching the stadium. Without a valid match ticket, that was as close as you were ever going to get. At Heysel, although there was no shortage of police and barking dogs and metal barricades, it appeared as though they were there for a separate event entirely; they didn't intervene in our lives in any way.

A similar absence of familiar basic procedures prevailed at the decrepit, archaic turnstiles. Had there been stewards or police immediately beyond the turnstiles to deter people from either trying to break in without tickets or from using fakes, it would have paid great dividends. Again, that was the custom at home. Instead, a sea of forgeries swept through unchecked and unnoticed, some fans just offered cash or pushed through, and the word spread rapidly that tickets may not be entirely necessary to get in to this match. Our precious tickets that we had sweated to get hold of were relegated to optional extras. Once again, the message seemed to be "do as you please, we have no control, no idea and quite frankly no interest". Like children given too much freedom and not enough discipline, that freedom was abused by some.

Once inside the shambolic stadium, the ineffective control over ground admission, the apparent lack of expertise in handling a crowd and the magnitude of the occasion led to the inevitable result: utter chaos. More supporters were crammed into Blocks X and Y than there was room for.

By 7pm on match day, all of these factors conspired to leave many thousands of Liverpool supporters shoehorned into a shabby, sweltering, over-crowded terrace under a warm sun, with a collective air of indiscipline and the temporary suspension of usual match day patterns. An industrial quantity of alcohol had fired imaginations, deadened inhibitions and further fuelled the brooding undercurrent. And there, just a few feet away in the adjoining section of terrace beyond some flimsy chicken wire, was Block Z, not empty or neutral but occupied by rival supporters. That football fans will partake liberally if bars are open is one of life's constants. Their refusal to tolerate rivals in their midst is another. Football supporters are nothing if not territorial, and this was after all our end of the stadium. To some amongst the Liverpool supporters — those who have ingrained within them that dismal primal instinct for violence — the Italian proximity was inflammatory and, as the US military might put it, an intolerable violation of their territorial integrity. And Block Z, as yet by no means full, also held the blissful prospect of the extra space that our section so clearly lacked. And what was to stop us laying claim to it? — a handful of ill-trained police and a flimsy stretch of chicken wire.

Could you ever devise a more volatile cocktail at a football match? There was motive, opportunity, and no apparent deterrent — the conditions were perfect. In the circumstances, the only surprise would have been a trouble-free evening. And given an identical set of circumstances, there can be little doubt that had any other mass-supported major English club reached that final instead of Liverpool, their fans would have behaved exactly as Liverpool's did, if not worse. There would still have been confrontation, the ground would still have been a ruin, the wall would still have collapsed, and the same history would have been made.

Proper ticket allocation, good ticket control at the stadium approach and access points, effective crowd segregation inside, adequate policing and security arrangements, appropriate facilities and strictly enforced alcohol bans or restrictions: all these actions would have denied the opportunity for violence. 'Controlling the controllables', in business jargon. In failing so transparently in every single one of those basic areas, the authorities handed on a plate to the small thug element amongst Liverpool's contingent the sort of opportunity which they had properly been denied at home for years, and which in all honesty they never expected to see again. And when they saw it, a depressing handful tucked in like a beggar at a banquet.

And yet, and yet, even then, even at that late stage, after virtually everything that could have been done wrongly had been, the tragedy could still have been averted. All that was needed was for the police, inadequate in numbers and training though they were, to be quicker to recognise the blindingly obvious warning signs and take decisive action to separate the rival sets of fans and defuse the inflammatory, simmering eyeball-to-eyeball proximity, by forming a human barrier between the rival supporters and creating a buffer zone. It was the custom then, in England and almost everywhere else. They could then have maintained the buffer zone throughout the match, with the aid of reinforcements, or had the option of leading the Italian supporters out of Block Z to the other end of the ground where their own supporters were (and where they would have preferred to be anyway), which would also have allowed the Liverpool contingent to overflow into Block Z to ease the congestion. Instead, they became paralysed by indecision as the situation worsened, and when what a Belgian eyewitness in Block Z later described as "the incomprehensible panic of the Italians" took hold, the police merely herded the fleeing Italian fans at baton point back towards the trouble they were seeking to escape. The pressure on the flimsy, crumbly perimeter wall grew and grew, and finally, disastrously, proved too much, leaving the police to watch on helplessly as the results of their indecision swelled to monstrous proportions.

Liverpool in particular, and English football in general, took all the blame and responsibility. In the dock of public opinion, Liverpool's supporters stood alone, guilty without the need for a trial. But alongside them, shoulder to shoulder, belonged a host of others: the UEFA officials who nominated a venue unfit to host anything more tumultuous than a whelk stall; the Heysel Stadium management who knowingly, willingly and openly sold tickets for the Liverpool end of the ground to Italian supporters; the bar owners who against their better judgment, police advice and all known precedent remained open and serving alcohol throughout the day; the police, who displayed a complete lack of awareness or urgency in the face of blatant warning signs, and incomprehensible inertia when clear decisive action could still have saved the day; and the Juventus supporters who carried inflammatory flags and banners to the match, as well as at least one firearm (a starting pistol, as it turned out, but who was going to know that from a distance?), who destroyed perimeter fencing, fought with police and launched an attack on Liverpool's supporters from the running track around the pitch, yet somehow emerged with their reputations intact.

Weighed down by collective guilt, Liverpool's mass of genuine supporters felt utterly let down by the behaviour of the few at Heysel, whose lack of self-control brought appalling consequences for the Italian victims, but also besmirched their own club's proud name across Europe and brought shame, disrepute and universal vilification to each one of us that we have still not shaken off. For many years it deprived club and supporters of the most exciting, uplifting experience available — involvement in European football. As individuals we felt as though we had paid the price many times over. Every Liverpool supporter I know and have ever met was sickened that innocent people, fellow football fans there for the same reason as us, died at a football match, and that a small minority of our own fans had a large part to play in it. I don't know any Liverpool supporter who seeks to deflect responsibility for the actions of some of our supporters that night. But I still believe that the accusation that Liverpool's supporters killed 39 people that night is narrow and over-simplistic. As I said at the start, I didn't think the story had been properly told. Heysel is unfinished business.

The deaths at the Heysel were wholly and easily preventable. They were the obscene consequences of gross negligence, stupefying incompetence, criminal lack of forethought and a whole succession of people — from the decision to use the apology for a stadium to the ticket selling arrangements to the policing — failing to do their jobs properly.

Had they done so, ugly primitive tribal aggression would have been properly denied its stage, and the chain would have broken.

Tragically, it held.

THESE ARE THE NAMES OF THOSE WHO WENT, LIKE US, TO WATCH A FOOTBALL MATCH, AND NEVER RETURNED:

ROCCO ACERRA (29)
BRUNO BALLI (50)
ALFONS BOS
GIANCARLO BRUSCHERA (21)
ANDREA CASULA (11)
GIOVANNI CASULA (44)
NINO CERRULLO (24)
WILLY CHIELENS
GIUSEPPINA CONTI (17)
DIRK DAENECKY
DIONISIO FABBRO (51)
JAQUES FRANÇOIS
EUGENIO GAGLIANO (35)
FRANCESCO GALLI (25)
GIANCARLO GONNELLI (20)
ALBERTO GUARINI (21)
GIOVACCHINO LANDINI (50)
ROBERTO LORENTINI (31)
BARBARA LUSCI (58)
FRANCO MARTELLI (46)
LORIS MESSORE (28)
GIANNI MASTROLACO (20)
SERGIO BASTINO MAZZINO (38)
LUCIANO ROCCO PAPALUCA (38)
LUIGI PIDONE (31)
BENTO PISTOLATO (50)
PATRICK RADCLIFFE
DOMENICO RAGAZZI (44)
ANTONIO RAGNANESE (29)
CLAUDE ROBERT
MARIO RONCHI (43)
DOMENICO RUSSO (28)
TARCISIO SALVI (49)
GIANFRANCO SARTO (47)
AMEDEO GIUSEPPE SPALAORE (55)
MARIO SPANU (41)
TARCISIO VENTURIN (23)
JEAN MICHEL WALLA
CLAUDIO ZAVARONI (28)

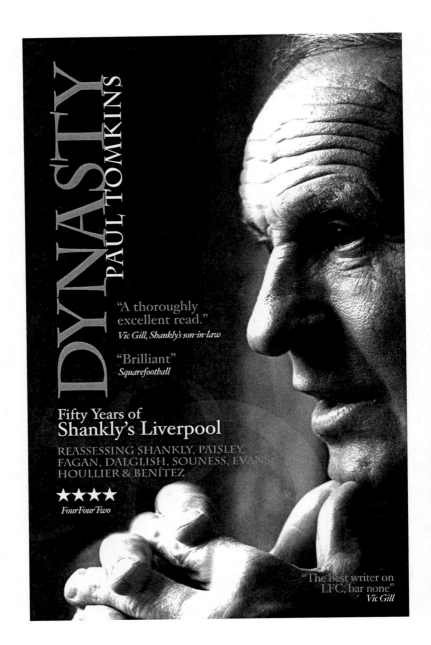

DYNASTY
PAUL TOMKINS

"A thoroughly
excellent read."
Vic Gill, Shankly's son-in-law

"Brilliant"
Squarefootball

Fifty Years of
Shankly's Liverpool

REASSESSING SHANKLY, PAISLEY,
FAGAN, DALGLISH, SOUNESS, EVANS,
HOULLIER & BENÍTEZ

★★★★
FourFourTwo

"The best writer on
LFC, bar none"
Vic Gill

- *ISBN* 978-0-9559253-0-6
- *RRP:* £9.99

www.paultomkins.com